EXPLORING SCRIPTURE

HOW THE BIBLE CAME TO BE

Rev. Phillip J. Cunningham, C.S.P.

PAULIST PRESS
New York and Mahwah, N.J.

Library of Congress Cataloging-in-Publication Data

Cunningham, Philip J., 1922-
    Exploring scripture: how the Bible came to be / Philip J. Cunningham.
        p.   cm.
    Includes bibliographical references.
    ISBN 0-8091-3295-8 (pbk.)
        1. Bible—Introductions.   2. Bible—History of contemporary events.   3. Bible—Study and teaching.   4. Bible—History of Biblical events.   I. Title.
BS475.2.C86   1992
220.6′1—dc20   91-38007
                                                                              CIP

Published by Paulist Press
997 Macarthur Boulevard
Mahwah, New Jersey 07430

Printed and bound in the
United States of America

Contents

iii

I. THE BEGINNINGS
FROM ABRAHAM TO MOSES (4000–1200 B.C.)

A. The New Stone Age (4000 B.C.)

B. The Middle Bronze Age (2050 B.C.)

C. The Late Bronze Age (1550 B.C.)

II. THE KINGDOM (1200–539 B.C.)
FROM DAVID TO THE EXILE

A. The Early Iron Age (1200 B.C.)

B. The Late Iron Age (900 B.C.)

C. Late Iron Age–Continued (700 B.C.)

D. The Babylonian Period (600 B.C.)

III. THE RETURN (539–63 B.C.)
FROM CYRUS TO POMPEY

A. The Persian Period (539–450 B.C.)

B. The Persian Period Continued (450–333 B.C.)

C. The Hellenistic Period

III. THE COMMUNITIES OF THE APOSTOLIC AGE: THESSALONICA, GALATIA, PHILIPPI

IV. THE PAULINE COMMUNITIES OF THE APOSTOLIC AGE: CORINTH

V. THE PAULINE COMMUNITIES OF THE APOSTOLIC AGE: CORINTH (Cont.), PHILEMON AND ROMANS

VI. THE PAULINE COMMUNITIES OF THE SUB-APOSTOLIC AGE: THE PASTORALS, COLOSSIANS AND EPHESIANS

VII. THE PAULINE COMMUNITIES OF THE SUB-APOSTOLIC AGE: LUKE AND ACTS

X. THE JOHANNINE COMMUNITIES

XI. THE FINAL DOCUMENTS OF THE NEW TESTAMENT

XII. FINALE

APPENDIX A

APPENDIX B

THIS BOOK IS DEDICATED IN LOVING MEMORY TO
MY MOTHER,
ELLEN THERESA CORRIGAN
1899–1989

EXPLORING SCRIPTURE

Preface

For twenty years I preached to and counseled Catholic students in a university setting. During that time I noted a significant change in their religious formation. As a result of the Second Vatican Council and of important improvements in catechetics, these students came to college life with a far broader acquaintance with scripture than had previous generations. A number of these young people read scripture every day.

Sadly, there is a down side in an otherwise fortunate development. The college student is now in an environment where the intellectual horizon rapidly expands. The student's awareness of science, history, art and literature increases but in a completely secular context, leaving his or her knowledge of the Bible isolated, in a vacuum, and lagging behind the student's general intellectual development. Some students may even feel that their religion itself is under attack.

Often as a result of such a perceived incompatibility between scripture and their newly acquired secular knowledge, some of these young people abandon not only their interest in the Bible but their religion as well. Others are attracted to one of the several well-staffed and well-financed student organizations who offer what purports to be a "non-sectarian" study of the Bible. Such groups are invariably *fundamentalist* in character and have a broader agenda than simply the Bible, seeking, in fact, to involve the student in a particular religion. In extreme cases, the student becomes enmeshed in a cult with disastrous consequences.

In light of what I have just described, it was my policy to

capitalize on the students' interest in scripture while at the same time broadening their understanding of the Bible's formation and literary content. Most importantly, I tried to show the relationship between history and the Bible's creation over the centuries: how it came into existence and how it relates to other forms of literature. Put another way, I tried to expose the students to the human context of the sacred scriptures while at the same time emphasizing the Bible's unique religious character. I felt that if young people could see the Bible in relationship to their newly acquired general information, their interest in scripture and in religion would not be diminished.

This book is a distillation of my efforts while at The Johns Hopkins University in Baltimore, Maryland, and at the University of California's San Diego campus to place the Bible in its historical context. I will be concerned with content only in so far as it reflects the context. Thus the strokes are broad and the reader is encouraged to pursue further the study of the sacred texts in the many excellent commentaries now available.

Though my focus was on the college student in the initial formation of the material for this book, I feel that those of any age and circumstance who are interested in deepening their appreciation of the Bible will profit from my approach. This would be especially true for those who have not yet seen how recent biblical scholarship has enriched our understanding of the sacred texts.

It is customary for the Christian to speak of the Bible as divided into an *Old* and a *New* Testament. More correct would be to speak of the *Hebrew Bible* rather than of an "old" Testament which could perpetuate an unfortunate Christian bias that regards the Old Testament as being superseded by the "New" and thus rendered passé. In truth, we cannot really understand our Christian scriptural heritage without an appreciation of the great gift given to us by the Jewish people, who were, as they still are, "the people of the Bible."

Though I have drawn the material for this book from many teachers and authors over the years, I would like to acknowledge a particular debt to the superb scholar and teacher, Father Raymond Brown. His lectures in the 1960s and his many books and articles introduced me to the wealth that lay in modern scripture scholarship. If this book has any merit, it can be, in a large part, attributed to him. The faults, however, are mine.

Finally, I want to express my appreciation to Christine Nelson who patiently read, corrected and improved the manuscript, to fellow Paulist, Larry Boadt, who guided me through the editorial process, and to the students and others who patiently sat through my sermons and talks as I groped toward the understanding and appreciation of the Bible which has enriched my life. I only hope their lives were enriched as well.

Part One
THE HEBREW BIBLE

THE CHRONOLOGY OF THE HEBREW BIBLE'S DEVELOPMENT

DATES (B.C.)	PENTATEUCH	PROPHETS	WRITINGS	HISTORY
—1000				
	Yahwist Source			
—900				
	Elohist Source			
—800				
		The Classical Prophets: Amos Hosea Isaiah I Micah		
—700				
	Yahwist and Elohist Sources Combined	The Pre-Exilic Prophets: Zephaniah Nahum		
	Deuteronomist Source	Habakkuk Jeremiah		
—600				
	Priestly Source	Exilic Prophets: Ezekiel Deutero-Isaiah		Deuteronomist History: Joshua, Judges 1,2 Saumel 1,2 Kings
		Lamentations		

8

THE CHRONOLOGY OF THE HEBREW BIBLE'S DEVELOPMENT

DATES (B.C.)	PENTATEUCH	PROPHETS	WRITINGS	HISTORY
—500				
	Combination of the Yahwist, Elohist, Deuteronomist and Priestly Sources into the Pentateuch	The Post-Exilic Prophets: Tritero-Isaiah Haggai Zechariah Malachi Obadiah	Job	
—400				
		Joel	Jonah Proverbs Psalms	1,2 Chronicles Ezra Nehemiah
—300				
			Ecclesiastes Tobit*	
—200				
			Sirach* Esther Daniel Judith* Baruch*	
—100				
			Wisdom*	1,2 Maccabees*

* These works are not included in the Hebrew Bible, but are in the Greek Septuagint (see pages 73ff) and are known as the Deuterocanonicals or the Apocrypha (see pages 76ff).

9

Introduction

THE WRITER AND LANGUAGE

Every author, no matter how technical his work, reveals himself in what he writes. Even more, he reveals his time and his culture. For example, had we only the works of Charles Dickens from the period, we could reconstruct a very accurate picture of the Victorian age and of Dickens himself. This would be true of almost any literature of any period. On the other hand, our knowledge of an historical era greatly enhances our appreciation of its literature. Knowing what we know of the Victorians and of Dickens himself gives us greater understanding of his masterpieces.

The reason for the above observation is not obscure. The writer must use the language he shares with his time and culture. How else could he speak to his contemporaries? Even though the author may have a profound influence on that language, as, for example, Dante had on Italian, the writer is himself very much a part of the historical context that embraces his language, just as Dante is very much part of the early Renaissance. This relationship is very dynamic and creative. The poet, especially, pushes language to its limits and thus is a force in creating that language. We have only to recall the contribution of Shakespeare to English to see the truth of this.

We now come to something remarkable about language. No matter how remote the period or strange the culture, we can translate its literature into our own language. There are exceptions such as the Mayan and related Central American languages where a living link with the past has been lost and the written form of the tongue cannot be translated. However, when we decipher the Sumerian cuneiform and the ancient Egyptian hieroglyphics, we do gain an insight into the times and cultures of these remote peoples which is detailed and which we relate to our own experiences.

HUMAN UNITY

What is revealed in these discoveries is the fundamental unity of human experience. Not a few authorities hold that all literature is, or could be, universally translatable because it is founded on a shared genetic base. The structure of language is "built in." It is also possible that all human language descends from a common "mother tongue" which originated in Africa, an area wherein the human race itself is generally thought to have arisen. My point is that literature, no matter how foreign or strange, falls within a shared human context.

THE ROLE OF TRADITION

There is a further point to be made about the formation of literature. In modern times, our paradigm for authorship is the writer at his desk (or computer) preparing the book which is then taken to the printer and which, ultimately, appears on the market. The book then takes on a life of its own. However, some ancient works are the product of a more complex process. We might more properly speak of their authors as communities, for they encapsulate the traditions of a people. The role of such traditions in the tribe, people or nation is beautifully summed up in the song "Tradition" from the musical "Fiddler on the Roof." Fundamentally, they are the source of the society's unity. A people preserves its traditions in its laws, folk songs, stories, remembered events, art work, handicrafts, and, most importantly here, in its literature.

In the ancient world where books were unknown or rare, the

actual writing down of these traditions usually came after a long period of oral transmission. Homer's *Iliad* and *Odyssey* are examples of such a process. Of course, an author may expand and enhance the traditional material in his literary creation. Wagner did just this in using old Germanic myths in composing *The Ring.* James Joyce, in his *Ulysses,* interweaves into the story, set in turn-of-the-century Dublin, material from the myths, folklore and legends found in the whole of western civilization.

THE BIBLE AS A WRITTEN TRADITION

In the past we have spoken of the Hebrew, Protestant, and Catholic Bibles. Modern scholarship makes no such distinctions. Scripture scholars of these faiths share a common body of research and generally agree upon conclusions as to the background and meaning of the sacred texts. For the Jew there is only "The Bible," which will be referred to as the Hebrew Bible. For the Christians the Bible includes an "Old" and a "New" Testament, with the Old Testament corresponding, more or less, to the Hebrew Bible. As we will see later, the form of the Bible used by the Roman Catholic Church includes material not found in the Hebrew Bible or in the Protestant Old Testament.

The Bible presents us with an excellent example of what we have been saying about traditional literature in general. The Greek word "biblia" is properly translated as "books," which in turn comes from "byblos," meaning "papyrus," an early material used in the making of manuscripts. Today the Bible is a compact, small library usually bound into a single volume. However, for most of their history, the sacred scriptures were a collection of scrolls that had been laboriously copied from the originals. Until the discoveries made in the Judean desert in 1947 at Qumran of the library of an Essene monastery, only fragments existed of these scrolls. The bound book or "codex" familiar to us originated in the fourth century of our era.

The Bible is a collection of documents containing a remarkable variety of literary forms including history, legend, stories such as folk tales, fables, parables and allegories, speeches, poetry, song lyrics and some forms that do not have a modern equivalent. These forms preserved the traditions that have roots going back to the dawn of civilization. The actual process of creating what we recognize as the Bible today took place over several hundred years and in widely differing historical circumstances, as we shall see.

LITERARY FORM

We can examine the Bible as we would any literary creation, looking at the relationship to its contemporary culture and historical period. Such an approach to ancient documents is called "historical criticism," a method which uses the techniques of both historical and literary criticism. As employed here, "criticism" does not have a negative implication. It means to examine the literary work by asking such questions as: Who is the author or authors? When and where was it written? What form of literary work is it (history, poetry, fiction, etc.)? Why was it written? What sort of background does it have? "All such preliminary questions help much in the comprehension of the biblical writing as something that comes to us from a definite literary context, time, and place in antiquity" (Joseph J. Fitzmyer, S.J., "Historical Criticism: Its Role in Biblical Criticism and Church Life," *Theological Studies,* June 1989, p. 249).

HISTORICAL CRITICISM AND BELIEF

To those who regard the Bible as a sacred text containing the revealed word of God, historical criticism presents a challenge. Studying these writings as one would study any human document seems to some a disregard of, or even a threat to, their true, supernatural character. Is there any need for such a purely literary understanding? After all, generations of the faithful have been moved and inspired by its contents without any such sophisticated understanding of the Bible's sources or circumstances of composition.

Protestants and Jews have long been encouraged to read the Bible for their own religious benefit, and since the Second Vatican Council a similar practice has been promoted among Catholics. If one holds the Bible to be the word of God, would not subjecting it to the criteria by which one judges other literary works be superfluous, if not disrespectful? Cannot God's message reach the reader of the Bible directly? Are the results of a scientific investigation into the text of any but academic interest?

FUNDAMENTALISM

Those who reject the historical-critical approach or who regard it as completely peripheral to a meaningful understanding of sacred scriptures are usually referred to as "fundamentalists." In its plainest form, fundamentalism relies on the literal meaning of the sacred text even when that text is a translation of an original language. As an example, if the Bible states that creation took place over a period of "seven days," then there were seven twenty-four hour days.

On the other hand, a moderate fundamentalist might accept that there were seven geologic periods or ages. In other words, there must be some correlation between the biblical text and history. Obviously, to either view, scientific examination of the text contributes little or nothing and the questions listed above would be of marginal interest at best. In effect, the fundamentalists isolate the Bible from the rest of literature. For the believer, such a separation is necessary. The Bible is "the word of God"; in the eyes of the faithful, its meaning must transcend a scientific analysis.

THE DIVINE REVEALED IN THE HUMAN

But can we ignore the human context of sacred scripture? Would this not be to neglect something equally *fundamental?* We read: "So God created humankind in his image, in the image of God he created them; male and female he created them" (Gen 1:27). Is there not a sense in which the divine is revealed in the human not in any crudely anthropocentric manner, such as through an idol or as a god in human form, but through the human without distorting the human?

In the view that will be reflected in this book, the God of Israel speaks to his people through the patriarchs, through Moses and through the prophets. God's words came to his people within human history, in actual times and places and involving real persons. These real experiences became part of a tradition preserved in the rich array of literary forms. God's word has a human context. Knowledge of that context can hardly detract from the meaning of his word. On the contrary, it should enhance our understanding of what God has revealed.

THE BIBLE AND THE PEOPLE

There is another limitation to fundamentalism. The Bible is an example of something mentioned earlier. As in other ancient works of literature, the Bible preserves the traditions of a people. Prior to the appearance of the written word, this people passed down their traditions orally. Even when there is evidence of a specific author, usually unknown, he sees himself as transmitting the beliefs of his contemporaries. The fact that such an author's work is incorporated into the Bible is evidence of this. We speak of the people of the Bible. We might equally speak of the Bible of the people. They compiled the sacred text, preserved and protected it. Their culture and history cannot be completely irrelevant to the understanding of God's word. After all, they were God's people. In effect, the fundamentalist's denigration of the scientific exploration of sacred scripture impoverishes rather than enriches our appreciation of God's word.

LIMITS TO HISTORICAL CRITICISM

To reject the fundamentalist approach to scriptures is not to say that the historical-critical method has been without problems. When first introduced in modern times over two centuries ago, the method was flawed by the influence of extremely rationalistic philosophies and limited archeological data. The initial tendency was to "throw the baby out with the bath." The proponents of such criticism were skeptical of any historical validity to the Bible and allowed little, if any, role for religion in scientific speculation. Not surprisingly, the more traditional Christian and Jewish groups rejected the conclusions of the historical-critical method.

In time, as the use of this method was modified by later proponents using the results of archeological findings and as its conclusions became less radical, historical criticism became the keystone of modern scripture scholarship. Far from proving to be deleterious to a religious understanding of the Bible, such scholarship has been beneficial. Admittedly, the Catholic Church came late to this realization. However, in two encyclical letters, *Divino Afflante Spiritu* (1943) and *Humani Generis* (1950), Pope Pius XII encouraged Catholic scripture scholars to employ this modern method of studying the Bible.

Both the Bible and science speak of the origins of the universe and of mankind. Much of the debate between historical criticism and the various forms of fundamentalism centers here. The heated and touchy public debate over evolution, especially its teaching in the public schools, demonstrates the current importance of how the believer, as well as the unbeliever, views the sacred texts. Appendix A contains one approach to this controversy.

STUDY QUESTIONS

1. What is the relationship between language and culture, and why will this be important in our understanding of the Bible?
2. What role does tradition play in many forms of ancient literature?
3. What is a brief description of the Bible?
4. What is "historical criticism" and how would it be used to understand the Bible?
5. What is "fundamentalism" in regard to understanding the Bible?
6. What is meant by the "human context" of the Bible?

I

The Beginnings
From Abraham to Moses (4000–1200 B.C.)

A. THE NEW STONE AGE (4000 B.C.)

- The Rise of the Sumerian Civilization in Eastern Mesopotamia
- The Rise of Civilization Along the Nile
- The First Year of the Jewish Calendar (3750 B.C.)
- Beginning of the Early Bronze Age (3200 B.C.)
- Origin of Cuneiform, the Earliest Form of Writing (c. 3200 B.C.)
- Gilgamesh, Legendary King of Uruk (c. 2750 B.C.)
- Cheops, Builder of the Great Pyramid (2700 to 2675 B.C.)
- Semitic Amorites Begin Their Migration into the Fertile Crescent (c. 2500 B.C.)

1. The Beginning

SUGGESTED READING: GENESIS, CHAPTERS 1–11

An analysis of the opening chapters of the book of Genesis reveals the roots of the biblical people to be in the Sumerian culture. (See Appendix A.) It is there also that their story begins with one Abram, son of Terah, born in Ur of the Chaldeans (11:27ff). God speaks to Abram, later to be called Abraham: "Now the Lord said to Abram, 'Go from your country and your kindred and your father's house to the land that I will show you. I will make of you a great nation, and I will bless you, and make your name great, so that you will be a blessing . . . and in you all the families of the earth shall be blessed' " (12:1–3).

Abraham was most likely the dimly remembered founder of a nomadic tribe who led his people along the ancient trade routes of the Fertile Crescent of Mesopotamia. The main road led from the cities along the Tigris and Euphrates, north and then west to the Mediterranean where at a crossroads highways went north up the coast and south to Egypt. It will be on this stage that the history of the people of the Bible will be played out.

2. Mesopotamia

A crow flying due east from the Nile delta would cover a thousand miles in reaching the delta of the Tigris and Euphrates rivers where they empty into the Persian Gulf. For most of the time the crow would be traversing deserts: the Arabian, Negev and Sinai. However, in an arc that rises from the Persian Gulf, follows the Tigris and Euphrates north, then curves west along the foothills of the mountain ranges lying to the north, the Zagros and the Taurus, and finally turns south along the Mediterranean coast to reach the Nile delta, we have the Fertile Crescent of Mesopotamia, an area that can justifiably be called the womb of western civilization.

With the advent of agriculture in the Neolithic period (7000 to 4000 B.C.), village life began. These small population centers were often found on the banks of rivers, especially as primitive irrigation was developed. As the age ended, the Nile basin and the watershed of the Tigris and Euphrates became well inhabited and may have been in contact since there is evidence that these centers traded with one another. During the Bronze Age (3200 to 1550 B.C.) humanity took a giant step forward with the introduction of writing which seems to have originated with these early efforts to engage in trade.

The Sumerians entered eastern Mesopotamia at the beginning

of the fourth millennium and organized the area into a group of city states. Their cuneiform writing, incised on clay tablets, is the earliest we have. These records give us a picture of the dawning of civilization. It was a civilization, however, marked by instability and change. The Tigris and Euphrates, fed by melting mountain snows and intermittent storms, are singularly erratic. Fierce storms roared out of the mountains, and general floodings of the whole region are documented in ancient records. As one might expect, the mythology of the Sumerians was uncommonly violent in character.

Added to these destabilizing problems were the periodic invasions of populations from the surrounding areas, no doubt attracted by the wealth of the emerging cities; one dominant group was frequently replaced by another. In fact, by the beginning of the second millennium, the Sumerian peoples themselves disappeared from history. Beginning around 2500 B.C. a migrant group known as the semitic Amorites began to emerge from the Arabian and Syrian deserts, living as a nomadic people on the outskirts and rural areas of the Fertile Crescent. Among them were the ancestors of the people of the Bible.

3. Egypt

At almost the same time, another primitive civilization was growing up on the banks of the Nile. Its written language was in hieroglyphics, preserved for us on the walls and monuments of their cities, as well as on papyrus, the earliest form of paper. Surrounded by deserts, the civilization of the Nile was relatively isolated. The river that was its lifeline is still noted for the regularity of its rise and fall. These two factors may account for the stability that characterizes the ancient history of the Nile basin, so much so that we can speak of its civilization simply as Egyptian. From the earliest days, these two population centers were linked by bustling trade routes.

B. THE MIDDLE BRONZE AGE (2050 B.C.)

- Stonehenge Is a Center of Worship in England
- Abram Leaves Ur in Chaldea
- The Period of the Patriarchs (1900–1700 B.C.)
- Hammurabi, King of Babylonia
- The Hyksos Form a Kingdom in the Nile Delta (1700 to 1600 B.C.)

1. The People of the Bible

SUGGESTED READING: GENESIS 11:27–14:24; CHAPTERS 37–46

The people of the Bible belonged to a semitic group called the Amorites that began to move into the basin of the Tigris and Euphrates at the middle of the third millennium B.C. The stories told in Genesis (chapter 12ff) about the patriarch Abraham, his relatives and children contain many details reflecting what we know of the Fertile Crescent in that period. He was the leader of a clan or tribe that moved along the trade routes between eastern Mesopotamia and Egypt, living not much differently from the Bedouin of today. Their means of transport and trade item, as well, was the donkey. The camel had not yet been domesticated. Abram's name and adventures became part of the folklore belonging to a group of interrelated tribes that eventually settled in the territory known as the land of Canaan, roughly in the northern part of modern Palestine—a name which is a variation of "Philistine," an ethnic group occupying the area at the end of the second millennium B.C. In the Roman empire, it was the province of *Syria Palestina.*

By the middle of the second millennium, some of the ancestors of the people of the Bible had migrated into Egypt and prospered there during the ascendancy of a series of non-Egyptian rulers, the Hyksos—Egyptian for "foreign rulers." These were an Asian and partly semitic people, so the "descendants of Abraham" would have "fitted in" and even gained some prominence. The lore surrounding Abraham's great grandsons, Joseph and his brothers (Genesis, chapters 37–47), reflects what we know of the Hyksos period in Egypt.

C. THE LATE BRONZE AGE (1550 B.C.)

- Invention of the First True Alphabet (Old Canaanite) (c. 1500 B.C.)
- The Hyksos Are Expelled from Egypt (1500 B.C.)
- Ikhnaton (Amenhotep of Egypt, Husband of Nefertiti) Sets Up Aton, the Sun God, as the Only God (1385 B.C.)
- Tutankhamen, After Brief Reign, Is Entombed (1350 B.C.)
- Rameses II (1290–1224 B.C.) and Menepbah (1224–1214 B.C.), Rulers of Egypt
- Moses and the Exodus from Egypt (c. 1290 B.C.)
- The Israelites Enter the Land of Canaan (1220 B.C.)
- First Mention of the Israelites in History (1207 B.C.)
- The Period of the Judges of Israel (1220 to 1050 B.C.)

1. Moses

SUGGESTED READING: EXODUS, CHAPTERS 1–14

In 1550 B.C., the native Egyptians overthrew their Hyksos rulers and established a new dynasty. The passage in Exodus (1:8), "Now a new king arose over Egypt, who did not know Joseph," may reflect the change in the fortunes of the immigrant populations. Some must have left; others, remaining in Egypt, fell into little more than slavery. We know that such oppressed peoples were used by Rameses II (1290–1224 B.C.) to carry out his enormous building projects, the impressive ruins of which can still be seen today.

Now arises the figure that dominates the Hebrew Bible. Abraham can be said to be the father of his people in a physical sense. However, Moses is, without doubt, the spiritual father of the people of the Bible. His name in Egyptian means ". . . is born," as in "Rameses," i.e. "Ra is born." Only in the case of Moses the name of the Egyptian god is omitted, giving substance to the tradition that the great leader of his people had been raised by Egyptian parents and only later in life became identified with enslaved countrymen. It was he who mobilized and led a group of oppressed slaves out of Egypt and into the Sinai desert. However we evaluate the biblical description of this event, it can truly be labeled "miraculous," the *tour de force* of one of history's great leaders. We can also attribute to Moses the three unique features of the religious heritage he left to his followers.

2. Moses' Contribution

a. The One God

No doubt during their period of enslavement, the people of the Bible preserved some memory of their tribal gods. Like their neighbors, they were polytheistic, but owed their allegiance to a particular god, "El Shaddai," the "God of the Mountain." Traces of this usage are found in Genesis (17:1; 28:3; 35:11; 43:14; 48:3), Exodus (6:3), and Ezekiel (1:24; 10:5). English translations usually render "Shaddai" as "the Almighty." However, it was through Moses that the people were first told of "Yahweh." The meaning of the name is obscure. "He who is" may be as close as we can come. What is important is that Yahweh is the God who freed his people from slavery, who cares for them and is now guiding them on the return to their homeland. The people did not cease to believe in the existence of other gods, but Yahweh was the most powerful of the gods and, above all, he was *their* God.

It is interesting to note that a century before Moses, the pharaoh of Egypt, Ikhnaton, attempted to establish Aton, the sun god, as the only god. On his death and during the brief reign of Tutankhamen (King Tut) the pantheon of Egyptian deities was reestablished. Monotheism will become a belief of the people of the Bible only much later. Nevertheless, the monotheism that characterizes not only Judaism, but both of the other great religions of the west, Christianity and Muhammadanism, rises upon the foundation laid by Moses.

b. The Covenant

Moses told his followers that as Yahweh's chosen people they were bound to their God by a unique agreement or covenant. Cast in the form of a suzerainty treaty, the covenant resembled an ancient agreement that imposed obligations on both God and his people, much as a dominant ruler would bind himself to a subordinate people. As we read in the book of Exodus (20:2–3), "I am the Lord your God, who brought you out of the land of Egypt, out of the house of slavery; you shall have no other gods before me." As we shall see, the laws and customs that came to govern the people of the Bible in the later centuries will be added to the original covenant and be given the authority of the supreme "law-giver" himself, Moses.

c. The People of the Land

As we come to the end of the thirteenth century, Moses had led his people to the eastern borders of the land of Canaan after a forty year trek through the Sinai desert. Up to now, history can only discern the dim outlines of the people of the Bible intermixed as they were with other populations. Across the Jordan lay an area of mixed populations. The Canaanites themselves lived along the shores of the Mediterranean. Inland were villages and small city-states of disparate heritages. Among these were tribal groups related

to the descendants of Jacob but who had remained in Canaan.
Their presence greatly facilitated the invaders in their attempt to
dominate the land.

3. Joshua and the Judges

**SUGGESTED READING: JOSHUA, CHAPTERS 1–12;
JUDGES, CHAPTERS 6–8**

A stele or memorial stone now in the Cairo museum records
the military exploits of the pharaoh, Merenptah (1212–1202). Incised on it is, "Canaan has been plundered into every sort of
woe. . . . Israel is laid waste and his seed is not." This claim of
victory is the earliest record we have of the Israelites. The biblical
books of Joshua and Judges record the struggle of Moses' followers
to gain a foothold in the land of Canaan. Though the picture these
books give of Israel's achievement is idealized to and includes legendary material, it is meant to reflect the conviction that it was
Yahweh who gave them the promised land. Moses himself, as tradition has it, died before his people crossed the Jordan.

As the conquest of Canaan proceeded under Moses' successor,
Joshua, the land was divided loosely and appropriated among the
tribes who took their names from the twelve sons of Jacob who had
been given the name "Israel" as we read in Exodus (35:10). Though
at first nomads, the "Israelites" began to settle on the land and
eventually moved into villages and cities. They maintained their
tribal relationships through an *amphictomy* which was a unity
around a central religious shrine. Eventually, the shrine of the Israelites was established at Shiloh and contained the "ark of the covenant." A description of the ark is found in Exodus (25:10–22). In it
were the original tablets of the law given to Moses. The shrine
became the symbol of Yahweh's presence with his people.

As the book of Judges relates, the presence of the Israelites in
Canaan did not go unchallenged. As various crises arose, Yahweh
summoned leaders from his people, the "judges," to meet the

threats to their survival. One such leader was Gideon, another was Samson. The period of the judges lasted from 1200 to 1050 B.C. when the Israelites faced a new and greater challenge.

STUDY QUESTIONS

1. Who was Abram?
2. What is the Fertile Crescent and how did the Nile basin differ from it?
3. What event is thought to be connected with the stories of Joseph and his brothers?
4. How does history picture Moses and his achievement?
5. What was Moses' contribution to the understanding of God?
6. What was the covenant and what did it eventually include?
7. What is the central point stressed by Joshua and Judges?
8. How were the tribes of Israel organized after they occupied the land?
9. What purpose was served by the persons known as the "judges"?

II

The Kingdom (1200–539 B.C.)
From David to the Exile

A. THE EARLY IRON AGE (1200 B.C.)

- With the Destruction of Troy, the Trojan War Ends (1193 B.C.)
- Saul Is Chosen as King of Israel (1020 B.C.)
- David Becomes King of Judah and Israel (1000 B.C.)
- Jerusalem Becomes the Capital of the Combined Kingdom (c. 1000 B.C.)
- Solomon Succeeds David and Reigns from 967 to 928 B.C.
- The Division into Judah and Israel, the Northern and Southern Kingdoms (928 B.C.)
- Samaria Becomes the Capital of the Northern Kingdom
- The formation of the Yahwist and Elohist sources

1. The Philistine Threat

SUGGESTED READING: 1 SAMUEL 1:1–28; 8:1–10:1

The "peoples of the sea," as the Philistines were called, came out of the northwest from the Aegean about the same time as the Israelites were entering Canaan from the east. Repulsed by the Egyptians, the Philistines established themselves on the coastal plain that runs along the western Mediterranean. Conflict between these two invading populations was not long in coming. The Philistines had the crucial advantage of iron weapons. Soon the Israelites were being driven back into the hill country.

The loose organization of independent tribes was no match for this new enemy as their resistance to the Philistines tended to be piecemeal. A single leader was needed to unite the tribes and, as we read in 1 Samuel (8:5), the Israelites wanted a king. The request is more radical than it might seem, since up to now Yahweh himself had been regarded as the king of Israel who ruled through his chosen vicars. A king would rule in his own right and, as 1 Samuel (8:11–18) makes clear, things would be very different for then on.

Saul, a member of the tribe of Benjamin, was the first to be chosen as king. At first Saul was successful in his military campaigns. However, he was defeated by the Philistines and perished along with his sons in 1000 B.C. The man who was to succeed Saul as king is second only to Moses as a pivotal character in the subsequent history of the people of the Bible.

2. David, the King

SUGGESTED READING: 1 SAMUEL, CHAPTERS 16–31; 2 SAMUEL, CHAPTERS 1–13

David's meteoric rise from shepherd to king is one of the most familiar stories in the Hebrew Bible, memorialized in art and literature. No other personage in the Old Testament is as vividly drawn. David ended the threat of the Philistines and successively defeated the other enemies of the kingdom. He first ruled in Judah, the area embracing southern Palestine. Subsequently he became the king of all the Israelites and expanded the territory under their control.

The most enduring contributions to the history of Israel were David's conquest of Jerusalem and the establishment of that city as the nation's capital (2 Sam 5). Very likely with the purpose of reinforcing the influence of Jerusalem, David had the ark of the covenant moved into the city, making it the religious as well as administrative center of the nation (2 Sam 6).

According to custom, David was designated king by an anointing (2 Sam 2). The use of oil to symbolize the passing on of power was common in the ancient world. The Hebrew word for "anointed" is "messiah." In later centuries, the hope for the restoration of an "anointed king," a "messiah," will become part of the dream sustaining the people of the Bible in their darkest hours. However, for the present, the Israelites enjoyed the first measure of peace and prosperity they had ever known. Looking back, God's people would idealize the memory of these years as their "golden age."

3. Solomon

SUGGESTED READING: 1 KINGS, CHAPTERS 2-13

David's forty year reign ended peacefully in 961 B.C. and his son Solomon succeeded to the throne. During his reign, Israel reached the apex of its power and influence throughout the Middle East. Tribute poured in from all sides as the nation became a strategic trading center. To reflect this new-found prominence, Solomon embarked on an ambitious building program. The "edifice complex" seemed to have afflicted most of the rulers in the ancient world and not a few in modern times as well.

Unfortunately, power and prosperity had a down side. The wealth was not equally distributed. Few were rich and the rest lived in grinding poverty. To increase the efficiency of conscription for military service and for taxation, Solomon reorganized the country into twelve administrative districts. Soon there was considerable unrest, partly fueled by the onerous burden of conscriptions and taxation, and partly by Solomon's involvement with idolatrous religions.

4. The Two Kingdoms: Israel and Judah

SUGGESTED READING: 1 KINGS, CHAPTERS 12-16

Though Solomon was able to hold the rebellious elements in check, his son Rehoboam could not. Shortly after the death of

Solomon, the ten northern divisions of the country revolted and chose their own king, Jeroboam I. The city of Samaria became the capital of the northern kingdom which retained the name Israel, and its southern counterpart became known as Judah. Divided and frequently at odds with each other, the chosen people will soon confront the folly of their rivalry.

5. The Formation of the Pentateuch Begins

SUGGESTED READING: GENESIS, CHAPTERS 1–4, 9, 11

a. The Tradition

At the time of the split between the northern and southern kingdoms, their peoples must have shared a rich tradition, dating back over a millennium: Sumerian myths, legends about the patriarchs, the heritage of Moses and the life in the desert, laws from these earlier times and subsequent accretions, remembrances of the period of Joshua and the judges, court records of Saul, David and Solomon, prayers, rituals and hymns from the temple celebrations. Some appreciation of the wealth of the nation's heritage can be seen in the earliest examples we have, such as the Song of Deborah found in Judges (5:2–31) and the psalms attributed to King David. The beautiful story found in the book of Ruth also originated in the time of David, but was probably put in written form centuries later. All this was to form the matrix from which the Pentateuch would begin its formation.

The Pentateuch (in Greek, "[the book of] five volumes") is made up of the books of Genesis, Exodus, Leviticus, Numbers, and Deuteronomy. In Judaism it is called the "Torah," meaning "law." These books have a complex history. Existing in earlier forms, they were subsequently modified before becoming the versions we have today. Biblical scholarship is able to discern the presence of these earlier forms and to determine the historical periods they represent. It is customary to refer to these primitive forms as "sources" or "traditions." Whether they existed as documents or were preserved orally is difficult if not impossible to determine. However, the sources enable us to relate the Pentateuch's development to the history of the people of the Bible.

b. *The Yahwist Source*

Just prior to or just after the separation of Judah and Israel the first phase of the Hebrew Bible's formation began in the southern part of the nation. At that time, traditional material was woven into the primitive sources which modern scholarship calls the "Yahwist"—the name coming from its use of God's proper name, "Yahweh." Other traditions hold that the divine name was not revealed until God spoke to Moses as told in Exodus (3:14); seemingly unaware of that fact, the Yahwist source uses "Yahweh" from its very beginning.

The Yahwist source reflects the nationalism resulting from the victories of David and from the power and prosperity of Solomon's reign. As the glory of the nation begins to fade, the Yahwist tradition emphasizes God's promise of salvation, seeing it repeatedly renewed throughout the stories of the patriarchs. The twelve sons of Jacob symbolize the unity of the nation, and Judah is presented as the leader of that fraternity. Finally, when the nation's existence was threatened, the Davidic monarchy with its source in the southern kingdom is shown to be the fulfillment of Yahweh's saving promise to his people. The people and places mentioned in the Yahwist source also tend to be associated with the southern kingdom.

There are other characteristics of the Yahwist tradition. It has a strong narrative style, vivid and realistic. The deity is anthropomorphic; Yahweh walks, talks, reprimands, punishes; he is very much one of the actors in the drama of human history, a history he determines. In Genesis we find vividly recounted the creation and fall of Adam and Eve, the fratricide of Cain (2:4-4:16), Noah's disgrace at the hands of his son (9:18-27), and the ultimate disintegration of human unity at the tower of Babel (11:1-9)—all seen as preparatory to God's saving action which begins with the story of Abraham.

c. The Elohist Source

When the northern kingdom, Israel, became independent of the south, a similar tradition also began to develop. As with the Yahwist source this tradition is named by modern scholars from the word used for the deity, "Elohim," the plural form of the semitic "El." Why a plural form was used to designate the God of Israel is not clearly known. The proper name of God, "Yahweh," being revealed only at the time of Moses is not used in the Elohist source until then.

The Elohist source, as you might expect, reflects the outlook of the northern kingdom, showing more interest its own heroes, Jacob, Joseph and Joshua. Stylistically, there are less anthropomorphisms in dealing with the deity, and as a result the divinity is more remote in its relationship to humanity.

For the remainder of the tenth century, through the ninth and into the eighth, the Yahwist and Elohist sources were developed and handed down. The traditions would have been transmitted orally and in written form, though we have none of these early manuscripts. Meanwhile, the rivalry between the two kingdoms drove them further and further apart, eroding their strength as a terrible threat arose at the other end of the Fertile Crescent.

STUDY QUESTIONS

1. What prompted the Israelite desire for a king?
2. What were the achievements of David?
3. What later became the significance of David's being an "anointed king"?
4. What tragedy followed the reign of Solomon?
5. What is the Pentateuch and where and when did the traditions it

contains begin? What is the "Yahwist source"? What is the "Elohist source"? How do these sources differ?

B. THE LATE IRON AGE (900 B.C.)

- The Iliad and the Odyssey Are Composed by Homer
- First Recorded Olympic Games (776 B.C.)
- The Advent of the Classical Prophets:
    Amos (760–750 B.C.)
    Hosea (c. 750–725 B.C.)
    Isaiah I (742–687 B.C.)
    Micah (750–687 B.C.)
- The Traditional Founding of the City of Rome (753 B.C.)
- Tiglath-pileser III Comes to Power in Assyria (745 B.C.)
- The Northern Kingdom Ceases To Exist (721 B.C.)

1. The Rise of Assyria

Now the sleeping giant in eastern Mesopotamia began to stir. After centuries in eclipse, the Assyrians started to expand their influence toward the west. By the mid-ninth century B.C., the ruler of Israel was paying tribute to stave off annexation. In the following century, under the rule of Tiglath-pileser, half of the northern kingdom was absorbed into the Assyrian empire, and the ruler of Judah was forced to buy some measure of independence by paying tribute. Then, in 721 B.C., Samaria fell to the Assyrians who were led by Sargon II; the population of the northern kingdom was either dispersed or absorbed as other populations migrated into the area. Israel was no more. This is the origin of the "lost tribes of Israel." There was nothing unusual about their fate, as it was the custom of the Assyrians to deport and scatter conquered peoples and repopulate their lands with others.

Now Judah was all that remained of the once mighty kingdom founded by David; never again was that lost glory to be restored.

However, his rule and that of Solomon's were remembered as a golden age and its restoration hoped for by the people of the Bible. But the trauma that marked the demise of the northern kingdom was not without its blessing; it gave to subsequent generations the achievements of four remarkable men, the pre-exilic prophets. Before examining the achievements we will consider the nature of prophecy in the Near East during the Iron Age.

2. The Meaning of Prophecy in the Ancient Near East

It is a rare newspaper or news broadcast today that does not contain the prognostications of a modern prophet telling us what's likely to happen in economics, politics, sports and the like. As an advanced technological society, we constantly use our sciences to probe reality for clues that might predict the future. In a concern for the future, primitive cultures, either contemporary or ancient, do not differ from us; what they lack is the technology we employ to make our predictions.

With little or no scientific knowledge of why things happen, the primitive mind regards all of reality as the immediate handiwork of a god or of the gods. From this point of view, to know the future it is necessary for one to be able to discern the will of the god or gods. In the ancient Near East such discerners were known as "prophets," or, in Hebrew, "nabi." These seers are found as advisors to the rulers and leaders of many cultures that surrounded the people of the Bible. Not surprisingly, then, it is with the establishing of the monarchy in the time of Samuel, Saul and David that prophets appear in biblical history.

3. Biblical Prophecy

SUGGESTED READING: 2 KINGS, CHAPTERS 16–18

Though we know of individual prophets such as Samuel (1 Sam 3:1–21), Gad (1 Sam 22:5), Nathan (2 Sam 7:1–17), Elijah (1

Kgs 17:1–18), and Elisha (2 Kgs 2:1–18), other prophets from this period belonged to groups who made their living through prophetic utterance, often in an ecstatic frenzy. The focus of these prophecies was usually to determine what would be the consequences of a given decision. Thus they often were part of the leader's or ruler's entourage. Conflict between the "official" prophets and the biblical prophet is not uncommon.

With the beginning of the eighth century B.C. and its rising threats to both the northern and southern kingdoms, a distinctive form of prophecy known as "classical" makes its appearance. It is "the fearless revelation of the moral will of Yahweh the God of Israel's covenant that is to be characteristic of classical prophecy setting it apart from all other prophecy, both of Israel and its neighbors . . ." ("Introduction to Prophetic Literature," by Bruce Vauter, C.M. in *The New Jerome Biblical Commentary,* p. 190a). Though it has its roots in the earlier prophets, the focus of classical prophecy on Yahweh's moral will is its distinctive mark.

4. Classical Prophecy

It is with classical prophecy that we first encounter the voices of individuals through writings by or about them. Though some of the classical prophets were reluctant to assume the formal title of "prophet," each professed to speak for Yahweh. Their words are not theirs, they say, but are those of the Lord God. Yet this divine inspiration does not absorb the speaker, suppressing his humanity or individuality. Quite the contrary, it is the deep humanity and striking individuality of each of the prophets which gives us the richness and variety we find in their writings. In part, their writings achieve such a distinctive character by employing a diverse array of literary forms—poetry, song lyrics, dramatic dialogue, legalese, even symbolic action—in which to communicate the divine message.

True, the works attributed to them have undergone changes in the long period of transition to their final form, but they are rooted in concrete personages who reflect on the challenges facing the people of the Bible from the eighth through the fourth centuries. Thus, these men provide us with a most significant insight into the formation of the Hebrew Bible. Further, their works will be extremely influential in the composition of the New Testament.

In the eighth century B.C., while the kingdom of Israel still existed, the earliest of the classical prophets can be divided between those who were active in the northern kingdom, Amos and Hosea, and those of the southern kingdom, Isaiah and Micah.

a. Amos

SUGGESTED READING: THE BOOK OF AMOS

We begin the era of the classical prophets in the northern kingdom, Israel, during the mid-eighth century, a time of peace and prosperity. For the moment, there was no threat either from eastern Mesopotamia or from Egypt, and the periodic struggle with the southern kingdom of Judah was quiescent. However, the words of the prophet recorded in the book of Amos reveal a society decaying from within as he inveighs against the social injustices of his time in the strongest terms: "They sell the righteous for silver, and the needy for a pair of sandals—Ah, you that turn justice to wormwood, and bring righteousness to the ground . . . you trample on the poor . . ." (2:6; 5:7–11). Wealth had divided the nation into the very rich and the very poor, destroying the more egalitarian society of an earlier age. "Hear this, you that trample on the needy, and bring to ruin the poor of the land" (8:4).

We know little of Amos, save that he came from Tekoa in Judah and was both farmer and shepherd, not a professional prophet. "I am no prophet, nor a prophet's son; but I am a herdsman, and a dresser of sycamore trees, and the Lord took me from following the flock, and the Lord said to me, 'Go, prophesy to my people Israel' " (7:14–15). Responding to God's call, Amos went to the northern kingdom where he was heard and his words were preserved, testimony to the power of his prophecy.

He accuses the Israelites of relying on their special status as God's chosen people to exempt them from the punishment due their crimes. Further, Amos admonishes them that their religious rituals have degenerated into a superstition, rendered meaningless by their failure to reform. "Even though you offer me your burnt offerings and grain offerings, I will not accept them . . . let justice roll down like waters, and righteousness like an everflowing stream" (5:22–24). They will not escape Yahweh's wrath. "The eyes of the Lord God are upon the sinful kingdom, and I will destroy it from the face of the earth" (9:8).

Still the vision of Amos is not a hopeless one. At the close of the biblical record of his prophecy there is a note of hope. "I will not utterly destroy the house of Jacob, says the Lord. . . . On that day I will raise up the booth of David that is fallen, and repair its breaches, and raise up its ruins, and rebuild it as in the days of old" (9:8–11). Some two centuries later, when Jerusalem lies in ruins, the survivors in exile will cling to the book of Amos with its promise of restoration.

b. Hosea

SUGGESTED READING: THE BOOK OF HOSEA

We come now to the final days of Israel, the northern kingdom. The monarchy has been unstable, plagued by a series of assassinations. The power of Assyria moves steadily closer. To preserve itself, Israel has entered into foreign alliances rather than place its trust in Yahweh. Further, a fratricidal war with Judah, the southern kingdom, has sapped the strength of both.

All these failings are reflected in the book of Hosea. They are oracles the prophet uttered between 750 and 732 B.C., reflecting what he regarded as the most serious failing of his people—idolatry. By this time the people of the Bible had been living on the land for centuries. Like the farmers and herdsmen around them, their foremost concern was fertility. Only productive land, herds and families guaranteed survival in a harsh, demanding environment. The temptation to appeal to pagan gods for assistance was too much for many in Israel which meant engaging in the orgiastic rituals of their pagan neighbors, even incorporating such rites into the worship of Yahweh. "The men themselves go aside with whores, and sacrifice with temple prostitutes" (4:14). The pagan gods most frequently referred to are the "baals." The word means "Lord" and was a divine appellation that may have been given to a range of deities.

Hosea compares the faithlessness of Israel to that of his wife, who he says is an adulterous woman. Some regard this as an actual experience of Hosea. If so, it is the only biographical information we have about the prophet other than the fact that he lived in the northern kingdom. As the wife betrayed her husband, so has Israel abandoned Yahweh. "I will no longer have pity on the house of Israel or forgive them" (1:6), Yahweh calls upon Israel to reform. "Or I will strip her naked . . . and make her like a wilderness, and turn her into a parched land, and kill her with thirst" (2:3). The very fertility that Israel hoped to gain by idolatry will be taken away.

Though Hosea's oracles are often harsh, seeming to forego any possibility for the future, he does hold out hope in the end. "Afterward the Israelites shall return and seek the Lord their God, and David their king; they shall come in awe to the Lord and to his goodness in the latter days. . . . The people of Judah and the people of Israel shall be gathered together" (3:5; 1:11). As with Amos before him, Hosea holds out hope for a future restoration, again a promise that will encourage exiles in the times to come.

   c. Isaiah

SUGGESTED READING: THE BOOK OF ISAIAH, CHAPTERS 1–39

As we have seen, the kingdom of Israel was destroyed in 721 B.C. However, before this occurred, prophets had also arisen in the southern kingdom of Judah. The words of the first and most prominent of these are contained in the book of Isaiah. Living in Jerusalem and moving easily among those making up the royal court, Isaiah flourished in the years 742–701 B.C. Thus he witnessed the annihilation of the northern kingdom, Israel, and the struggles of the southern kingdom, Judah, to survive the assaults of the Assyrians. It was a period of decline for his country, and the record we have of Isaiah's oracles reflects the prophet's characterization of that decline.

Isaiah saw the waning of Judah's power in the face of an external threat, not as simply military, political or economic, but as spiritual. In the face of the threat from Assyria, the people had lost their faith in the saving strength of Yahweh. They had abandoned him, making alliances with their pagan neighbors, even with Assyria itself. In the mouth of the prophet, Yahweh passes judgment on Judah. "Hear, O heavens, and listen, O earth; for the Lord has spoken: I reared children and brought them up, but they have rebelled against me. The ox knows its owner, and the donkey its master's crib; but Israel does not know, my people do not understand. Ah, sinful nation, people laden with iniquity, offspring who do evil, children who deal corruptly, who have forsaken the Lord, who have despised the Holy One of Israel, who are utterly estranged" (1:2–4).

As did Amos, Isaiah rails against the injustices that the rich have inflicted on the poor and needy. "It is you who have devoured the vineyard; the spoil of the poor is in your houses. What do you mean by crushing my people, by grinding the face of the poor?" (3:14–15). The prophet issues a call for reform before it is too late. "Wash yourselves; make yourselves clean; remove the evil of your doings from before my eyes; cease to do evil, learn to do good; seek justice" (1:16–17). But, apparently, his call fell upon deaf ears.

The prophet envisions the fate of Judah in apocalyptic terms. The word means "revelation," and as a literary form it will become common in Judaism after 200 B.C. Dealing as it does with the final period of world history, a period marked by catastrophic events, this style has its roots in the classical prophets when they look forward to the final fulfillment of Yahweh's promises. We can see an early example of this in Isaiah, "Now the Lord is about to lay waste the earth and make it desolate, and he will twist its surface and scatter its inhabitants. . . . The earth shall be utterly laid waste and utterly despoiled; for the Lord has spoken this word" (24:1–3).

But there is still hope, as Yahweh will not abandon the people he loves; mercifully, some will survive, if only a few. "A remnant shall return, the remnant of Jacob to the mighty God" (10:21). Isaiah holds out the hope of a restoration of their former grandeur. "In days to come the mountain of the Lord's house shall be established as the highest of the mountains, and shall be raised above the hills; all the nations shall stream to it" (2:2).

Speaking through Isaiah Yahweh promises that the Davidic line of kings will once more attain power and glory. "His authority shall grow continually, and there shall be endless peace for the throne of David and his kingdom. He will establish and uphold it with justice and with righteousness from this time onward and forevermore" (9:7). In the dark days that were to come, when Jerusalem was in ruins and there was no living heir to David's throne, the prophet's hope would sustain the people of the Bible.

Isaiah must be ranked as the most influential of prophets. When the Hebrew Bible reaches its final form, the book of Isaiah will be the first in the record of the prophetic writings. Moreover, a century and a half later another prophetic voice was heard, carrying on the tradition of Isaiah and referred to by modern scholars as Deutero-Isaiah. Chapters 40 to 55 of the book of Isaiah are attributed to this prophet who assumed the mantle of the original Isaiah. Later in the sixth century B.C., a third figure, Tritero-Isaiah, again spoke with the voice of Isaiah and contributed the final section (chapters 56–66) found in the collection attributed to the original prophet.

d. Micah

SUGGESTED READING: THE BOOK OF MICAH

Micah, a contemporary of Isaiah, came from a small village in Judah, not far from where the prophet Amos was born. Like him, Micah was born in a rural area that suffered much from the exactions of wealthy land owners. His oracles reflect this concern. "Alas for those who devise wickedness. . . . They covet fields, and seize them; houses, and take them away; they oppress householder and house, people and their inheritance" (2:1–2). He has equally harsh words for Judah's rulers, priests and professional prophets. "Its rulers give judgment for a bribe, its priests teach for a price, its prophets give oracles for money" (3:11). For this injustice and venality Judah will meet the fate of the northern kingdom. "Therefore because of you Zion shall be plowed as a field; Jerusalem shall become a heap of ruins" (3:12).

Like Hosea, Amos, and Isaiah before him, Micah looked ahead to a restoration of power and glory. "In days to come the mountain of the Lord's house shall be established as the highest of the mountains, and shall be raised up above the hills. Peoples shall stream to it, and many nations shall come and say: 'Come, let us go up to the mountain of the Lord, to the house of the God of Jacob' " (4:1–2).

We hear also in Micah the promise of a future ideal ruler who will guide the people of the Bible to the fulfillment of Yahweh's promises. "But you, O Bethlehem of Ephrathah . . . from you shall come forth for me one who is to rule in Israel . . . for now he shall be great to the ends of the earth" (5:2–4). David, the symbol of Judah's golden age, came from Bethlehem; thus Micah sees the survival of the Davidic line as crucial to Judah's hopes.

STUDY QUESTIONS

1. What is the tragic occurrence of 721 B.C.?
2. What is prophecy in the ancient Near East and how does this
   form of prophecy first appear in the Hebrew Bible?
3. When do the "classical prophets" appear and what makes them
   distinctive?
4. What events accompanied the appearance of Micah and what
   was his reaction?
5. What most troubled Hosea and what literary device did he use
   to express his condemnation?
6. How did Isaiah see the threat to Judah?
7. What was the remedy that Isaiah proposed?
8. What are the complaints that Micah voices?
9. What does Micah envision for the future?

C. LATE IRON AGE–CONTINUED (700 B.C.)

- The Acropolis of Athens Is Begun
- The Final Days of Judah
    Conflation of Yahwist and Elohist Sources
    Deuteronomist Source Formed
- King Josiah of Judah (640–609 B.C.) Attempts Social and Re-
  ligious Reforms
    Zephaniah (640–630 B.C.)
- Nineveh Falls and the Assyrians Are Defeated by the Babylo-
  nians (612–610 B.C.)
    Nahum (612 B.C.)
- Jehoiakim Ascends the Throne of Judah (609 B.C.)
    Habakkuk (605–597 B.C.)
    Jeremiah (628–587 B.C.)

1. The Final Days of Judah

SUGGESTED READING: 2 KINGS, CHAPTERS 22–25

Now it looked as if even the surviving remnant of the people of the Bible would not long exist but would ultimately share the fate of the northern kingdom and disappear from history. However, as the Assyrians continued their march toward Judah they found themselves under attack from the rear. A resurgent Babylon rose in revolt, and in the ensuing struggle Judah, along with other vassal states, chose to ally itself with its conquerors, the Assyrians, a most unfortunate choice. In 612 B.C. Nineveh was conquered and Assyria itself was swept from history. The victorious Babylonians were not likely to look kindly on Assyria's former allies, including Judah.

2. Conflation of the Yahwist and Elohist Source

After the destruction of the northern kingdom in 721 B.C., the survivors fled to the south, joining the remaining people of the Bible in Judah. The ruler at that time, Hezekiah (715–687 B.C.), was attempting a reform of the religious life of his people. The refugees brought with them their own traditions, including the Yahwist source, as well as laws, rituals and traditions, many of which were different from those of Judah.

In the next hundred years there were several significant stages in the development of the Hebrew Bible. For one, the Yahwist and Elohist sources combined. Since the conflation of the two biblical sources was done in Judah, its source was favored, so when the material coincided, the Elohist was preferred. As we saw earlier, only the differences in style and content enable us to distinguish these sources today.

3. The Formation of the Deuteronomist Source

SUGGESTED READING: DEUTERONOMY, CHAPTERS 5, 6, 30, 32 and 34

As one might expect, the destruction of the kingdom of Israel and the loss of the ten northern tribes was a traumatic event, challenging the conviction of the Judeans that their God was all-powerful and that he was faithful to his promises, especially that of guaranteeing his people's possession of the land. As the noose of Assyrian power pressed in on the shrunken enclave of Judah, Yahweh's guarantees seemed all the more problematic.

Matters were only made worse by the growing corruption of Judah's society in spite of efforts at reform. The people were becoming increasingly involved in the paganism that surrounded them, particularly with the fertility cults. Altars dedicated to the gods of Assyrians were to be found in the temple itself. Could Yahweh have abandoned his people because they had first been unfaithful to him? Apparently some priests and prophets came to just such a conclusion and began a recasting of the tradition in its light.

4. The Deuteronomist Source and the Book of Deuteronomy

The Deuteronomist source is most evident in the book of the Pentateuch bearing that name. "Deuteronomy" means "copy of the law," and that is what it appears to be, covering as it does events between the Israelites' departure from Mount Horeb (Sinai) to the death of Moses and the accession to leadership of Joshua. As with the Yahwist and Elohist sources, the Deuteronomist source includes legislation attributed to Moses. These laws, however, reflect more the conditions of city life in the pre-exilic period than the circumstances of the rural scene that characterize the earlier sources.

What makes the Deuteronomist source distinctive is its strong moral tone. Toward the end of the book of Deuteronomy in a discourse attributed to Moses, the future of the people of the Bible is to be determined by their faithfulness to the laws of Yahweh. "See, I have set before you today life and prosperity, death and adversity. If you obey the commandments of the Lord your God that I am commanding you today, by loving the Lord your God, walking in his ways . . . you shall live and become numerous, and the Lord your God will bless you in the land that you are entering to possess. But if your heart turns away and you do not hear, but are led astray to bow down to other gods and serve them, I declare to you today that you shall perish" (30:15–18).

Some written form of the Deuteronomist source was apparently discovered in the temple precincts when King Josiah of Judah began his efforts at religious reform in 621 B.C. The document must have exerted considerable influence on the king's attempt to restore a covenant spirit to God's people. Unfortunately the respite resulting from the Babylonian challenge to Assyria was drawing to a close. Josiah himself perished in battle in 609 B.C. Darkness was soon to fall upon the surviving people of the Bible.

5. Seventh Century Prophets

a. Zephaniah

SUGGESTED READING: THE BOOK OF ZEPHANIAH

In spite of the impending threat, or perhaps because of it, the Judeans drifted from the worship of Yahweh. They may have felt that Yahweh had abandoned them, and they turned to the apparently more powerful deities of the pagans. The book of Zephaniah warns that Yahweh's anger had been roused by the faithlessness of his people as they turned to the worship of foreign gods, particularly the baals. The prophet's warning is the gravest. "I will utterly sweep away everything from the face of the earth, says the Lord. . . . I will make the wicked stumble. I will cut off humanity from the face of the earth. . . . I will stretch out my hand against Judah, and against all the inhabitants of Jerusalem" (1:2–4).

The prophetic voice of Zephaniah also protested the corruption and pro-Assyrian policies of those who ruled Judea as regents during the minority of King Josiah. "The officials within it [Jerusalem] are roaring lions; its judges are evening wolves. . . . Its prophets [the professional prophets who advised the ruler] are reckless, faithless persons; its priests have profaned what is sacred" (3:3–4).

Yet for Zephaniah the situation was not without hope. In spite of the terrible punishment Yahweh will inflict, he still promises to relent. "At that time I will bring you home, at the time when I gather you; for I will make you renowned and praised among all the peoples of the earth, when I restore your fortunes before your eyes, says the Lord" (3:20). However, it will only be a small number who will survive this holocaust. "For I will leave in the midst of you a people humble and lowly. They shall seek refuge in the name of the Lord" (3:12). Later, when survivors return to the ruins of Jerusalem, they will see in what has happened to them the fulfillment of Zephaniah's oracle and be encouraged to look to their future with hope.

b. Nahum

SUGGESTED READING: THE BOOK OF NAHUM

We know little more than his name, but when the Assyrians were defeated by the Babylonians in 612 B.C., the prophet Nahum gloats over their fate, seeing Yahweh as triumphant. "A jealous and avenging God is the Lord, the Lord is avenging and wrathful" (1:2). Now God's people have reason to rejoice and to return to the sole worship of Yahweh. "Look! On the mountains the feet of one who brings good tidings, who proclaims peace! Celebrate your festivals, O Judah, fulfill your vows" (1:15). He must certainly have been expressing the feelings of relief of his fellow Judeans as the threat to their very existence seems to have been so fortuitously removed.

c. Habakkuk

SUGGESTED READING: THE BOOK OF HABAKKUK

Unfortunately, as we have seen, Babylon proved an even greater threat than Assyria and exultation soon turned to gloom. As the century ended Judah's prospects were bleak indeed. The prophet Habakkuk cries out in desperation. "O Lord, how long shall I cry for help, and you will not listen? Or cry to you 'Violence!' and you will not save?" (1:2). The prophet sees the impending doom as God's punishment for the continued injustice inflicted on the poor and defenseless. "So the law becomes slack and justice never prevails. The wicked surround the righteous—therefore judgment comes forth perverted" (1:4). If the vision of the book of Habakkuk is bleak, it is because Judah's very existence is now in what must have appeared to be its final hours. But it is not despairing. "Yet I will rejoice in the Lord; I will exult in the God of my salvation" (3:18).

d. Jeremiah

SUGGESTED READING: THE BOOK OF JEREMIAH, CHAPTERS 1, 2, 30 AND 31

The prophet Jeremiah answered Yahweh's call in 628 B.C. His oracles and writings make up the longest book of the Bible and give us the most detailed picture we have of a prophet's life. During the reign of Josiah, Jeremiah supported the reforms instituted by the ruler by calling his fellow countrymen to a greater faithfulness to the words of Yahweh. "But this people has a stubborn and rebellious heart; they have turned aside and gone away. They do not say in their hearts, 'Let us fear the Lord our God' " (5:23).

With the ascendancy of Jehoiakim and the subsequent falling away of the Judeans from the reforms of Josiah, Jeremiah becomes a fiercer critic of both the people and their rulers. "Thus says the Lord: Record this man as childless, a man who shall not succeed in his days; for none of his offspring shall succeed in sitting on the throne of David, and ruling again in Judah" (22:30). Theirs is a faithlessness that merits total devastation. "I will make Jerusalem a heap of ruins, a lair of jackals; and I will make the towns of Judah a desolation, without inhabitant" (9:11).

His criticism and pessimistic outlook earned him the hostility of the ruling faction who were trying to move the people to resist the encroachments of Babylon. Jeremiah appeared to be sapping the will to fight. But his message was not one of hopelessness. The chosen people of Yahweh were promised a future. "In those days the house of Judah shall join the house of Israel, and together they shall come from the land of the north to the land that I gave your ancestors for a heritage" (3:18). And that land would be ruled by a restored Davidic dynasty. "The days are surely coming, says the Lord, when I will raise up for David a righteous branch. . . . In his days Judah will be saved and Israel will live in safety" (23:5–6).

However, the unique element in Jeremiah's prophecy is the future relationship he envisions between Yahweh and his people. In the past, the nation's ruler was key to God's dealings with his people, a relationship that might be described as something external or institutional. Now it will be different. "The days are surely coming, says the Lord, when I will make a new covenant with the house of Israel and the house of Judah. It will not be like the covenant that I made with their ancestors. . . . I will put my law within them, and I will write it on their hearts; and I will be their God, and they shall be my people" (31:31–33). When the monarchy is no more, Jeremiah's words will indeed be "prophetic."

STUDY QUESTIONS

1. What important event took place in the final days of the kingdom of Judah?

2. What new biblical source appears at this time and in what book of the Pentateuch does it first appear?
3. What is distinctive about this source?
4. What seems to have inspired Zephaniah's prophecy?
5. What fate does Zephaniah foresee for his people?
6. What does the prophet Nahum celebrate?
7. What change of Judah's circumstances do we see reflected in Habakkuk?
8. What change in the conduct of two of Judah's rulers do we find influencing the writing of Jeremiah?
9. What change does Jeremiah predict in the relationship between Yahweh and his people?

D. THE BABYLONIAN PERIOD (600 B.C.)

- The Mayan Civilization Rises in Central America
- Rome Is Declared a Republic
- The "Fables" of Aesop
- Nebuchadnezzar Defeats the Egyptians at Carchemish (605 B.C.)
- The Babylonians Conquer Judah and the First Group of Exiles Leave for Babylon (597 B.C.)
- The Exilic Prophets:
    Ezekiel (597–591 B.C.)
- The Babylonians Conquer and Destroy Jerusalem and the Exile Begins (587 B.C.)
- Pythagoras, Philosopher and Mathematician (587–491 B.C.)
    Lamentations (c. 587 B.C.)
    Priestly Source Formed, Including Material Found in Leviticus and Numbers
    Deutero-Isaiah (550–549 B.C.)
- Siddhartha, the Gautama Buddha (550–480 B.C.)
    Deuteronomist History Formed, Including Joshua, Judges, 1 and 2 Samuel and 1 and 2 Kings

1. The Fall of Judah

SUGGESTED READINGS: 2 CHRONICLES, CHAPTER 36

Nebuchadnezzar defeated the Egyptians forces at Carchemish in 605 B.C. However, the Egyptians regained the upper hand in 601 B.C. Jehoiakim attempted to capitalize on these changing fortunes but ended up on the wrong side. Jerusalem was captured by the Babylonians in 597 B.C. and a large number of Judeans were taken off to exile in Babylon. The city, however, was spared. Unfortunately, Zedekiah, the last ruler of Judah, repeated his predecessor's mistake and, siding with the Egyptians, revolted against the occupying forces. Nebuchadnezzar besieged Jerusalem, conquering and destroying it in 587 B.C. The bulk of the population, certainly all the leading citizenry, were carried off to Babylon; an event subsequently referred to as the "exile." Anyone viewing the ruins and the few remaining Judeans clustered about them, living in abject poverty, would conclude this to be the final chapter in the story of the people of the Bible.

2. Lamentations

SUGGESTED READING: THE BOOK OF LAMENTATIONS

Once attributed to Jeremiah, the writings found in Lamentations are now thought to be by one or more anonymous authors. The five poems have left us a vivid picture of Jerusalem and its environs after the destruction of 587 B.C. "How lonely sits the city that once was full of people" (1:1). The author of the closing poem, however, prays that Yahweh will relent. "Restore us to yourself, O Lord, that we may be restored; renew our days as of old" (5:21). At the time of the writing there must have been little hope that the prayer would be answered.

3. The Exilic Prophets

As we have seen, the exile marked a traumatic change in the history of the people of the Bible. The two foundations upon which their religious and national life has rested since the time of David and Solomon, well over four hundred years, were the monarchy and the temple. (For some perspective, we should recall that four hundred years ago, our country was still occupied by the American Indians.) Now these two supports were gone and the outlook of the classical prophets begins to shift. Once their concern was the future of Israel and Judah and the threat of the faithlessness of God's people. Their expectations might be described as moral reform of both people and ruler and the survival of the nation.

From this nationalistic and concrete hope, we now see developing a more cosmic and universal expectancy. It will be more visionary and will be in more symbolic and allegorical terms. The readers of these prophets will be warned of an approaching cosmic catastrophe, a climactic conflict between Yahweh and evil, a day of the Lord. Only when the forces of good emerge from this struggle will the ultimate kingdom of Yahweh be established. As we noted earlier, such an outlook is called "apocalyptic."

a. Ezekiel

SUGGESTED READING: THE BOOK OF EZEKIEL, CHAPTERS 1–3, 37, 40–42

Though elements of the apocalyptic outlook are found in prophets that preceded him, it is in Ezekiel that we see them most clearly. Ezekiel was deported to Babylon in 597 B.C. and his writings date from 593 to 571 B.C. Much of the flavor of his work can be seen in his opening vision of Yahweh in all his glory (1:4ff). It is very reminiscent of a theophany of the ancient "storm god" augmented by numerous symbolic touches. Similarly, the "Vision of the Dry Bones" (37:1ff) and chapters 40–42 describing the restored temple show us Ezekiel's apocalyptic style.

Ezekiel saw the tragedy he witnessed as Yahweh's punishment for the faithlessness of his people. "I will scatter you among the nations and disperse you through the countries, and I will purge your filthiness out of you . . . you shall know that I am the Lord" (22:15–16). And, like his predecessors, he calls for repentance and a return to trust in Yahweh in the face of impending disaster. "Thus you have said: 'Our transgressions and our sins weigh upon us . . . how then can we live?' . . . Turn back from your evil ways; for why will you die, O house of Israel?' " (33:10–11).

Ezekiel still held out a hope for the future God's people, the restoration of the golden age under a Davidic ruler. "I will set up over them one shepherd, my servant David, and he shall feed them: he shall feed them and be their shepherd. And I, the Lord, will be their God, and my servant David shall be prince among them; I, the Lord, have spoken" (34:23–24). While descendants of David still existed, such a hope could be seen a realistic possibility. Later, with the extinction of the Davidic line, the expectation of a successor to David ruling Israel will take on a different character.

b. Deutero-Isaiah

SUGGESTED READING: THE BOOK OF ISAIAH, CHAPTERS 40, 42, 44:24–45:2, 49–55

As we reach the middle of the sixth century B.C., unbeknownst to the Exiles, their trial is about to end. At this critical point another prophetic voice is heard. Apparently a member of an "Isaian" school of religious thought, his words are included in the book of the prophet Isaiah, chapters 40 to 55. However, Deutero-Isaiah speaks to an audience different from his predecessor. The exiles are discouraged, destitute, and strongly tempted to apostasy. The prophet strives to bring to his countrymen a sustaining hope. "Comfort, O comfort my people, says your God. Speak tenderly to Jerusalem, and cry to her that she has served her term, that her penalty is paid" (40:1–2).

Deutero-Isaiah stresses the creative power of God. "I am the Lord, and there is no other. I form light and create darkness, I make weal and create woe; I the Lord do all these things" (45:6–7). "Sing, O heavens, for the Lord has done it; shout, O depths of the earth; break forth into singing, O mountains, O forest, and every tree in it! For the Lord has redeemed Jacob, and will be glorified in Israel" (44:23). Evidence of that saving power is seen by Deutero-Isaiah in the advent of Cyrus (see below). "Thus says the Lord to his anointed, to Cyrus, whose right hand I have grasped to subdue nations before him" (45:1). Because of the conqueror of Babylon a new exodus is to begin, bringing Israel once more to the promised land.

Four passages in Deutero-Isaiah make reference to a "servant of the Lord" (42:1–7; 49:1–7; 50:4–9; 52:13–53:12). The identity of this figure is much debated, but his sufferings are seen by Deutero-Isaiah as vital in the salvation of the people. "Surely he has borne our infirmities and carried our diseases . . . the Lord has laid on him the iniquity of us all" (53:4–6). These vicarious agonies are redemptive. "Because he poured out himself to death, and was numbered with the transgressors; yet he bore the sin of many, and made intercession for the transgressors" (53:12). Some speculate that the figure was Deutero-Isaiah himself who at the end of his life faced rejection by the very people he strove to comfort. In the period following the death of Jesus of Nazareth, his followers will find these passages from Deutero-Isaiah especially meaningful.

4. The Priestly Source

SUGGESTED READING: GENESIS 1:1–2:4

The Judeans exiled in Babylon faced an enormous challenge. The bases on which were grounded their culture and religion had either disappeared or were seriously eroded. They were no longer in possession of the land promised to them by Yahweh. The great temple and the holy city, Jerusalem, were gone, and, finally, the monarchy survived on the thinnest of threads. If the survivors were to preserve their heritage, a new understanding of that heritage had to be achieved.

A group of priests among the exiles assembled the cultic and legal traditions of both the northern and southern kingdoms. They had the lengthy genealogies that had been preserved as well as various legends that had been handed down. All of this became what scholars call the Priestly source, the final element that went into forming the Pentateuch.

As might be expected, the Priestly source places great stress upon the ritual guidelines, preserving the traditions of the temple worship. It also lays down the strictures governing the life of the faithful Jew, a code of conduct that would isolate the pious Israelite from the pagan world around him. We can see evidence of this in the book of Leviticus, which is entirely from the Priestly source, the name coming from the tribe of Levi which had been dedicated to the priesthood. As we saw in Deuteronomy, all of this legislation was attributed to Moses.

In its original form, the Priestly source may have been an alternate to that of the combined Elohist and Yahwist traditions, containing, in great part, the same material but with a different emphasis. The contrast between the two traditions can be seen by comparing the two creation accounts that begin the book of Genesis (1:1–2:4a and 2:4b–25). Following the end of the exile in 539 B.C., the Priestly source was combined with earlier traditions to give us the Pentateuch in substantially its present form.

5. The Deuteronomist History

As the Pentateuch was in the final stages of its formation, another crucial work of editing was taking place. The role of history in preserving a culture can hardly be overestimated. Facing the challenge of the exile, the survivors in Babylon sought to assemble the memories and records of their own past. Beginning where the

Pentateuch leaves off, the books of Joshua, Judges, 1 and 2 Samuel, and 1 and 2 Kings contain the history of the people of God down to the time just prior to the exile.

These books are not history in our sense, though they do contain facts about the past. Their purpose was to preserve and strengthen the faith of the people of the Bible. They gain much of their inspiration from the Deuteronomist source and are strongly influenced by the prophet Jeremiah as well. Trust in Yahweh and faithfulness to his laws as the true foundation of the people's hope for the future are played out in the history these books record. Failure, of both princes and people, to adhere to God's precepts have brought his people to their present sorry state. They will survive only if they regain their trust in Yahweh.

STUDY QUESTIONS

1. What is the subject of the book of Lamentations?
2. What changes in outlook are reflected in the exilic prophets?
3. Elements of what outlook are most prominent in the writings of Ezekiel?
4. With what hope does the work of Deutero-Isaiah open?
5. What important historical figure makes his appearance in Deutero-Isaiah?
6. Who is the "servant of the Lord"?
7. What source of the Pentateuch originates at this period and what are its characteristics?
8. What books of the Hebrew Bible are called the "Deuteronomist History" and what is their purpose?

III

The Return (539–63 B.C.) From Cyrus to Pompey

A. THE PERSIAN PERIOD (539–450 B.C.)

- Cyrus, Ruler of the Medes and Persians, Conquers Babylon (539 B.C.)
- Cyrus Issues a Decree Allowing the Exiles To Return to Judea (538 B.C.)
- Aeschylus, Greek Dramatist (525–456 B.C.)
- Socrates, Greek Philosopher (470–399 B.C.)
- Hippocrates, Greek Physician, "The Father of Medicine," is born (460 B.C.)
     Job (600–450 B.C.)
- Post-Exilic Prophets:
     Tritero-Isaiah (c. 515 B.C.)
     Haggai (c. 522 B.C.)
     Zechariah (520–518 B.C.)
     Malachi (c. 460 B.C.)
     Obadiah (c. 400 B.C.)
- Conflation of Yahwist, Elohist, Deuteronomist and Priestly Sources into Final Form of the *Pentateuch*

1. Cyrus and the Return

SUGGESTED READING: EZRA, CHAPTERS 1–5

Just as it seemed Israel would join the roster of vanished nations and peoples, a reprieve was granted. Cyrus, founder of the

Persian empire, conquered the Babylonians in a whirlwind campaign. In 539 B.C. he released the Jews exiled in Babylon and enabled them to return to Judea and rebuild the capital, Jerusalem, and its temple. The people of the Bible saw this as clear evidence of the salvation they had been promised. "(Yahweh) who says of Jerusalem, 'It shall be inhabited,' and of the cities of Judah, 'They shall be rebuilt' . . . who says of Cyrus, 'He is my shepherd, and he shall carry out all my purpose'; and who says of Jerusalem, 'It shall be rebuilt' " (Is 44:26-28).

In this post-exilic period, the people of the Bible, both those living in Judea and elsewhere, were referred to as "Jews." "Israel," when used, indicates the religious community. The survivors of the exile returned to a devastated land and to a future of vassalage, a pawn in the power struggle between empires. Their task of rebuilding would frequently appear to be an impossible dream. Many Jews did not return to Judah, and others, faced with the harsh conditions there, emigrated, marking the beginning of the diaspora, as Jews drifted out to the great cities and lived among nations of disparate cultures. Though the crisis of the exile had ended, the survival of the people of the Bible was still by no means assured.

a. Job

SUGGESTED READING: JOB, CHAPTERS 1, 2, 38, 39 AND 42

In the midst of the tragedy that surrounded the exile and return, an unknown Israelite author, drawing on the traditions and folklore of his people, fashioned a most remarkable dramatic poem which we know as the book of Job. It is the first book found in that section of the Hebrew Bible called "The Writings." Similar literature is found among the Egyptians and Babylonians, but the subject matter of Job is unique.

The traditional view of divine justice was that God rewarded the good and punished the evil. The hero of the book of Job has suffered a series of overwhelming disasters that have left him without family and possessions, and "loathsome sores . . . from the sole of his foot to the crown of his head" (2:7). Yet, "in all this Job did not sin or charge God with wrong-doing" (1:22). How then explain his sufferings?

Job and his three friends, Eliphaz, Bildad, and Zophar, debate the point at length, with Job maintaining his innocence and his friends insisting that his sufferings are evidence of his guilt before God. In the end, Job can only conclude that Yahweh's actions are a mystery. "I know that you can do all things, and that no purpose of yours can be thwarted. . . . Therefore I have uttered what I did not understand, things too wonderful for me, which I did not know" (42:2–3).

Those who underwent the defeat, the exile and, finally, the return to a shattered land certainly identified with the dilemma presented by Job. They could see in their tragedy a test of one's trust in God and a hope for restoration in the future, just as the hero of Job was restored to his former good fortune (42:12ff). The questions raised by Job have lost none of their force in the two and a half millennia since the book was written.

2. Post-Exilic Prophets

a. Tritero-Isaiah

SUGGESTED READING: ISAIAH, CHAPTERS 60–62, 65:17–25, 66

Shortly after the return of the exiles to a barren and shattered Judea and its capital city, Jerusalem, another prophetic voice is raised. His words are found in the final chapters of the book of Isaiah (56–66) and he is designated as Tritero-Isaiah. Like his earlier counterpart, Deutero-Isaiah, this writer was a member of an Isaian school of religious thought, adapting the vision of the founder to new crises. Now the Israelites were in their homeland,

and though they had seen Yahweh's promise fulfilled, the harsh, discouraging conditions they faced and their powerlessness caused their faith to weaken.

"Shout out, do not hold back! Lift up your voice like a trumpet! Announce to my people their rebellion, to the house of Jacob their sins" (58:1). Israel's leaders have failed. "Israel's sentinels are blind, they are all without knowledge. . . . The shepherds also have no understanding; they have all turned to their own way, to their own gain, one and all" (56:10–11). Vile, idolatrous practices of the worst sort have arisen. "Are you not children of transgression, the offspring of deceit—you that burn with lust among the oaks, under every green tree; you that slaughter your children in the valleys, under the clefts of the rocks?" (57:4–5).

The prophet calls for reform. "Is not this the fast that I choose: to loose the bonds of injustice . . . to let the oppressed go free . . . ? Is it not to share your bread with the hungry, and bring the homeless poor into your house; when you see the naked . . ." (58:6–7). If they respond to this call for justice, the prophet promises, "Then you shall take delight in the Lord, and I will make you ride upon the heights of the earth" (58:14).

Tritero-Isaiah opens up a new vision of Israel's future. "My house shall be called a house of prayer for all peoples. Thus says the Lord God, who gathers the outcasts of Israel" (56:7–8). To this vision of Yahweh as welcoming all peoples, the prophet adds a beautiful picture of an ultimate future. "Lo, I am about to create a new heavens and a new earth; the things of the past shall not be remembered or come to mind. Instead there shall always be rejoicing and happiness in what I create" (65:17–18). The peace and bliss of the new creation extends even to the animal kingdom. "The wolf and the lamb shall graze alike, and the lion shall eat hay like the ox. None shall hurt or destroy on all my holy mountain, says the Lord" (65:25). However the prophet does end on an apocalyptic note. "Lo, the Lord shall come in fire, his chariots like the whirlwind, to wreak his wrath with burning heat and his punishment with fiery flames. For the Lord shall judge all mankind by fire and sword"

(66:15–16). As with Deutero-Isaiah, this final Isaian voice may have found himself rejected by the returnees.

b. Haggai

SUGGESTED READING: THE BOOK OF HAGGAI

As the sixth century came to a close, the outlook for the returned exiles was bleak indeed. Judah occupied an area less than twenty square miles. The efforts at rebuilding the temple had so far only succeeded in constructing a new foundation. In the book of Haggai (c. 520 B.C.), we hear the prophet urging renewed effort at rebuilding the temple. "Is it a time for you yourselves to live in your paneled houses, while this house lies in ruins? Go up to the hills and bring wood and build the house, so that I may take pleasure in it and be honored, says the Lord" (1:4–8). The task, if undertaken, will be successful. "I will shake all the nations, so that the treasure of all nations shall come. . . . The latter splendor of this house shall be greater than the former . . . and in this place I will give prosperity" (2:7–9). His call was apparently effective, as the work was completed in 515 B.C.

c. Zechariah

SUGGESTED READING: THE BOOK OF ZECHARIAH, CHAPTERS 1, 9:9–17, 14

The prophet whose words are found in the book of Zechariah was a contemporary of Haggai. Writing in a highly visionary and symbolic prophecy Zechariah looked forward to a restored glory for Yahweh's people. "Many peoples and strong nations shall come to seek the Lord of hosts in Jerusalem, and to entreat the favor of the Lord. . . . In those days ten men from nations of every language shall take hold of a Jew, grasping his garment and saying, 'Let us go with you, for we have heard that God is with you' " (8:22–23).

Like his contemporary, Zechariah sought to encourage the

returnees and to spur their efforts at rebuilding the temple. He appears also to have given the people some hope for the return of a Davidic ruler. "It is he that shall build the temple of the Lord; he shall bear royal honor, and shall sit and rule on his throne" (6:13). The prophet also shares the apocalyptic vision of Isaiah and Ezekiel looking forward to a climactic end to history. "On that day . . . the Lord will become king over all the earth" (14:8–9).

d. Malachi

SUGGESTED READING: THE BOOK OF MALACHI

The book of Malachi gives a picture of life in Judea in the mid-fifth century. The temple is rebuilt but the people show its services little respect. "When you offer blind animals in sacrifice, is that not wrong? And when you offer those that are lame or sick, is that not wrong?" (1:8). The taking of foreign wives is not only a violation of the law, it is also a threat to the survival of the nation (2:11).

Again we hear the apocalyptic warning of an approaching "great and terrible day of the Lord" (4:5). It is a call to reform. "See, the day is coming, burning like an oven, when all the arrogant and all evildoers will be stubble. . . . But for you who revere my name the sun of righteousness shall rise, with healing in its wings" (4:1–2). These reforms will shortly be instituted under Ezra and Nehemiah (see below).

e. Obadiah

SUGGESTED READING: THE BOOK OF OBADIAH

Obadiah is the shortest of the prophetic books. It strikes the reader as harsh, vengeful and even overly nationalistic. The author gloats over the fate of the Edomites who occupied a territory adjacent to Judah. They had taken advantage of the tragedy in 587 B.C. to plunder the area that had been vacated by the exiles. The conquest of Edom by another Arabic population was regarded as an action of divine providence by the Israelites who were now struggling for survival. Ultimately the justice of God will triumph. "For the day of the Lord is near against all the nations" (v. 15).

3. Pentateuch

SUGGESTED READING: THE BOOK OF NUMBERS, CHAPTERS 1, 22–24

By the end of the fifth century, the Priestly source was interwoven with the already combined Yahwist, Elohist and Deuteronomist sources. This source can be found in parts of Genesis and Exodus, all of Leviticus, some verses of Deuteronomy and large sections of the book of Numbers. The latter book gets its name from the two censuses it records (1:20ff and 26:19ff). It also includes incidents from the desert period, intermixed with cultic and social legislation. The balance of Numbers is composed of independent traditions. It is at this point in history that the Pentateuch takes its final form. From now on, it will be the "torah," the "law," that will exert such a profound influence on God's chosen people as their future unfolds.

STUDY QUESTIONS

1. What resulted for the people of the Bible from Cyrus' conquest of Babylon?
2. What is unique about the book of Job?
3. What new vision of Israel's future is expressed in the section of Isaiah attributed to "Tritero-Isaiah"?
4. What were the circumstances in Judea at the time of Haggai and how did they influence his writing?
5. What views are expressed in the prophecy of Zechariah?

6. What does Malachi criticize and what are his visions of the future?
7. Why is Obadiah so harsh and vengeful toward the Edomites?
8. What occurs in the development of the Pentateuch at this time?

B. THE PERSIAN PERIOD CONTINUED (450–333 B.C.)

- Aristophanes, Comic Dramatist, Born 450 B.C.
- Sophocles, "Antigone" (443 B.C.)
- Euripides, "Medea" (431 B.C.)
- Plato, Greek Philosopher (427–347 B.C.)
- Aristotle, Greek Philosopher (384–322 B.C.)
- The Reforms of Nehemiah (c. 445 B.C.) and Ezra (c. 408 B.C.)
   1 and 2 Chronicles, Ezra and Nehemiah (c. 400 B.C.)
   Joel (400–350 B.C.)
   Jonah (c. 400 B.C.)
   Proverbs (c. 400 B.C.)
   Psalms (c. 400 B.C.)

1. The Period of Reform

SUGGESTED READING: THE BOOKS OF EZRA, CHAPTERS 7, 10:1–15 AND NEHEMIAH, CHAPTERS 1, 2, 6, 8

The return of the exiles did not miraculously restore them to their former glory. Despite the generally tolerant attitude of the Persians, Israel faced challenges from both within and without. Two men played crucial roles at this time: Nehemiah and Ezra.

Though a Jew, Nehemiah held an important post in the Persian court. Yet, moved by the plight of his people, he had himself appointed governor of Judah and journeyed to their desolated homeland to aid in its reconstruction (c. 445 B.C.). He saw the rebuilding of Jerusalem's walls as his most important task. Only then would it really be a city, something essential to restoring his countrymen's sense of identity. But, having reestablished governance for both city and countryside, Nehemiah saw his achievement threatened by the religious and moral decay of the people.

We are not sure of the date when Ezra comes to Jerusalem. A man versed in the law of Israel, Ezra set about the reform that Nehemiah recognized as essential to the future of the people of the Bible. The exact relationship between Ezra and the Pentateuch is not certain. What he used as the instrument of his reform may have been the books as we know them. In any event, from this point on the people of the Bible saw their religion as focused on the written word. As this spirit spread to the Jews of the diaspora, they were bound ever closer to their homeland as the center of their religious life.

2. The Bible Continues To Develop

a. 1 and 2 Chronicles, Ezra and Nehemiah

Sometime toward the end of the fifth century, these four books appear. Their dates and authorship are the subject of much scholarly debate. 1 and 2 Chronicles revisit the historical period covered by Samuel and Kings. However, the author, usually referred to as the chronicler, seeks to see in the story of David and his successors a reinforcement of the reforms introduced by Ezra: an emphasis on prayer and temple worship, ritual purity and faithfulness to the law. The role of priestly leadership is emphasized. The books reflect the changed conditions in which the Israelites now find themselves.

Ezra and Nehemiah take up the story of the people of the Bible at the end of the exile, covering their own time. Their purpose is not merely to relate what happened but to pass on their reforms to future generations. In these books and the two previous ones, we can see the early stages of the Jewish religion and culture as it will appear in the coming centuries. 1 and 2 Chronicles, Ezra and Nehemiah complete the historical works found in Hebrew Bible.

b. Joel

SUGGESTED READING: THE BOOK OF JOEL

As the fifth century closes we hear the voice of the prophet Joel, who brings classical prophecy to a close. A terrible plague of locusts in Judah has led the people to expect the imminent coming of the day of the Lord and Joel calls his people to repentance, "Rend your hearts and not your clothing. Return to the Lord, your God" (2:13). Only such a return will save them from utter destruction. Yet, God is merciful and this is the foundation for hope. "Then afterward I will pour out my spirit on all flesh; your sons and your daughters shall prophesy, your old men shall dream dreams, and your young men shall see visions" (2:28).

c. Jonah

SUGGESTED READING: THE BOOK OF JONAH

The work of an unknown author, Jonah is unique among the prophetic works. It is not the usual collection of sayings, but a narrative which is best described as a didactic parable, bearing some resemblance to an Aesop's fable. The trials of the hero Jonah are not without humor as he tries to avoid bringing God's message of repentance to Israel's traditional foes, the Assyrians. Jonah is further frustrated when, to his dismay, the people of Nineveh comply with Yahweh's request and are thus spared the destruction Jonah had obviously hoped would be their fate.

The author certainly meant the post-exilic Jews to see themselves in Jonah as narrow, vindictive and unforgiving. In the closing passage, Jonah bemoans the death of a plant that had sheltered him from the sun. Yahweh rebukes him: "You are concerned about the bush, for which you did not labor and which you did not grow; it came into being in a night and perished in a night. And should I not be concerned about Nineveh, that great city, in which there are more than a hundred and twenty thousand persons?" (4:10–11). The work is a warning to the Jews not to expect their God to ratify their prejudices.

d. Proverbs

SUGGESTED READING: THE BOOK OF PROVERBS, CHAPTERS 1, 8, 10

Proverbs is a collection of wise sayings. Some of the material could date as early as the reign of Solomon and certainly existed as an oral tradition for a long period. We do not know when the work was put in its final form or by whom.

One might title Proverbs "A Guide to Wise Living." Many of the sayings seem to have little if any religious content: "Go to the ant, you lazybones; consider its ways, and be wise" (6:6). "A soft answer turns away wrath, but a harsh word stirs up anger" (15:1). "It is better to live in a corner of the housetop than in a house shared with a contentious wife" (21:9).

During the post-exilic period, as the voices of the prophets were stilled and the difficult conditions of life made simple survival no easy task, the wise sayings of Proverbs, drawn from a rich tradition, would have come into prominence. In time they were put in their final written form.

e. Psalms

SUGGESTED READINGS: THE BOOK OF PSALMS, 1–10

No summary can do justice to the wealth of the collection of religious poetry we call the Psalms. Composed over a period of seven hundred years, some of the Psalms date back to the Davidic period, and a number of them may actually have been authored by the king himself. They reflect the numerous circumstances and cultures with which the people of the Bible were associated over the centuries and express a wide range of personal and communal spirituality and worship.

Periodically, collections were no doubt made of such poetry, some of which appear to have had musical accompaniment. Some final additions were made in the early post-exilic period, and we can assume that final collections of the collections must have been completed shortly after that time.

STUDY QUESTIONS

1. Who was Nehemiah and what was his achievement?
2. Who was Ezra and what was his achievement?
3. What is the chronicler seeking to do in his writings?
4. Under what circumstance is the prophet Joel writing?
5. What sort of a work is the book of Jonah and what is its purpose?
6. What development does the book of Proverbs reflect?
7. What makes up the book of Psalms?

C. THE HELLENISTIC PERIOD

- Alexander Defeats the Persians at Issus (333 B.C.) and dies in 323 B.C.
- Archimedes, Greek Mathematician (287–212 B.C.)
- The Punic Wars Between Rome and Carthage Begin (264 B.C.)
- Parchment Is Produced at Pergamum (250 B.C.)
- Hannibal Crosses the Alps (218 B.C.)
- The Great Wall of China (1,400 miles long) Is Built (215 B.C.)
- The Ptolemies Rule Judah (c. 300–200 B.C.)
    Ecclesiastes (c. 300 B.C.)
    Tobit (c. 200 B.C.)
- The Seleucids Rule Judah After 198 B.C.
    Sirach (190–180 B.C.)

- The Maccabean Revolt (167 B.C.)
    Esther (c. 150 B.C.)
    Daniel (c. 166 B.C.)
    Judith (175–135 B.C.)
    Baruch (200–100 B.C.)
- The Rule of the Hasmoneans (134–63 B.C.)
- Rome Conquers Greece (147 B.C.)
- Venus de Milo, Sculpture (140 B.C.)
- Cicero, Roman Politician and Orator (106–43 B.C.)
    1 and 2 Maccabees (c. 100 B.C.)
    Wisdom (c. 100 B.C.)
- Gaius Julius Caesar (100–44 B.C.)
- Spartacus, Leader of Slave and Gladiator Revolt, Is Defeated by Pompey and Crassus (71 B.C.)
- Pompey, the Roman General, Conquers Palestine (63 B.C.)
- Julius Caesar Is Assassinated (44 B.C.)
- Herod the Great Is Appointed King of Judea (40 B.C.)

1. Alexander the Great

Little is known of the Jews after the period of Nehemiah and Ezra (c. 400 B.C.) until the advent of Alexander the Great. Judah was allowed some measure of self-rule under their Persian overlords with administration in the hands of the priests who controlled the rebuilt temple. Archeology has uncovered traces of Jewish communities elsewhere in the Mideast, but that is all we know as we approach the events that will so radically change the ancient world.

Following the unification of Greece by Philip II of Macedon, his son and successor, Alexander (356–323 B.C.), defeated the Persians at Issus in 333 B.C. and took control of their territories. Eventually Alexander the Great established an empire that reached from Macedonia to India's Indus River, embracing the entire Fertile Crescent and extending into Egypt. There Alexandria still bears his name. On his death, Alexander's empire was divided among his generals.

The descendants of one of the generals, Ptolemy, ruled Egypt, and Judah was under their control until c. 199 B.C. when it was taken over by the Seleucids who governed Syria. The Ptolemies had been benign in their administration of Jerusalem and its environs, but not so the Seleucids. In 167 B.C. Antiochus IV (175–164 B.C.), after attempting the suppression of the Jewish religion, set up a altar to Zeus Olympios in Jerusalem's temple. This resulted in a open revolt led by the priest, Mattathias of Modein. He was followed in the leadership by his sons, Judas whose nickname was "Maccabee" or "Hammer." He led the revolutionaries from 167 to 160 B.C. followed by his brothers Jonathan (160–143 B.C.) and Simon (143–134 B.C.). In 142 B.C. Judah was given its independence by the Seleucid ruler, Demetrius II. The subsequent rulers, known as the Hasmoneans, expanded their control until it reached an expanse somewhat larger than present-day Palestine. This independence ended when the Roman general, Pompey, entered Jerusalem in 63 B.C., incorporating the territory into the Roman empire.

The struggle for power in the empire itself saw Julius Caesar (100–44 B.C.) defeat Pompey in 48 B.C. and be himself assassinated. After an interim of jockeying for dominance, Caesar's nephew Octavian became emperor in 30 B.C., taking the name Augustus. He ruled until 14 A.D. These struggles had ramifications in Palestine where the Hasmoneans sought to regain the power, but in the end they were replaced by Herod, an Idumaean (a non-Jewish group converted to Judaism in the previous century), who ruled from 37 to 4 B.C., and we are now on the threshold of the New Testament period.

These final three centuries before Christ saw the completion of the Jewish Bible and were marked by a struggle to preserve the Jewish heritage from its greatest challenge. The empire of Alexander the Great was not united only by military power. The culture of Greece, its language, philosophy, poetry, art, architecture and religion, spread to every corner of the regions under the control of Alexander and his successors. The force of the "Hellenistic" culture is amply testified to by its persistence even into our own time.

The efforts of Antiochus IV to establish the worship of the God who headed the Greek pantheon were only aspects of the attempt to replace a local culture with a universal one. Though that attempt failed, the struggle only shifted into other areas, in particular, the crucial element in culture language. Greek was rapidly becoming what it would be for the succeeding centuries, the *lingua franca* of the empire. Local tongues would continue to be used, but in business, government and education the universal language would be Greek. We can see this struggle as we look at the final books of the Hebrew Bible.

2. Ecclesiastes

SUGGESTED READING: THE BOOK OF ECCLESIASTES, CHAPTERS 1, 2 AND 12

The title is a translation of the Hebrew "qoheleth," meaning "one who convokes the assembly." Though the author is identified as "David's son . . . king of Jerusalem," possibly Solomon, this is apparently a literary device to lend authority to the work. Scholars place its composition around 250 B.C. during the rule of the Ptolemies. The Hebrew used is late, and there is a possibility of an original in Aramaic (see below).

The form of Ecclesiastes is that of a compilation of sage advice or popular wisdom and the tenor of the book can be seen in its opening lines, "Vanity of vanities! All is vanity!" (1:2) The work can be described as cynical, pragmatic, even pessimistic. It is certainly a challenge to any easy optimism about the human future: "What has been is what will be, and what has been done is what will be done; there is nothing new under the sun. Is there a thing of which it is said, 'See, this is new'? It has already been, in the ages before us" (1:9–10).

The presence of such a secular book in the Hebrew Bible is puzzling. A later editor must have thought so since he added a reminder to the reader, "The end of the matter; all has been heard. Fear God, and keep his commandments; for that is the whole duty of everyone" (12:13). However, during the rule of the Ptolemies, in the calm that preceded the storm, the people of the Bible may have needed a caution about taking God's providence for granted.

3. Divergent Traditions

The Hebrew Bible, as the name implies, was written in that language, a spoken tongue for many centuries. However, as time passed, spoken Hebrew was replaced by a related language, Aramaic. After the exile and with the diaspora, Jews living in various parts of the world used the local tongue, with Hebrew reserved for religious ceremony. Soon Hebrew became a "dead" language but remained in use for purposes similar to that of Latin in the Roman Catholic Church.

As Hebrew became a less familiar language, some Hebrew texts were translated into local languages, certainly into the Aramaic used by so many Jews. As we saw above in discussing Ecclesiastes, it is possible that some biblical material was first written in Aramaic and later translated into Hebrew when the book was accepted as part of the religious tradition.

Another candidate for translation was Greek. Certainly many of the Jews throughout the Mediterranean world made use of what we have already described as the *lingua franca* of the period. This would be particularly true for those who had a secular education and any degree of prominence in local society. Though up to this point no biblical text had been originally Greek, translations of parts of the Hebrew Bible into Greek existed, various books having been translated at different times by different people.

The process of grouping together the books of the Hebrew Bible had already begun. As we saw earlier, the Pentateuch had been formed by 400 B.C. During the third century B.C. the writings of the prophets and other biblical works were being brought together, not into bound volumes as we know them, i.e. "codexes," but were being joined together in continuous scrolls. Though substantial agreement between these collections existed, there were also variations. One such variation now in its early stages of formation will be of great significance in later centuries.

4. The Septuagint

Legend has it that seventy-two Jewish scholars, six from each tribe, were asked to make a Greek translation of the torah for the Alexandrian library during the reign of Ptolemy II (285–246 B.C.). The process was most likely much more complicated than that. The name traditionally given to this translation was the "Septuagint" from the Latin word for "seventy." Like all translations, the Septuagint is an interpretation of the Hebrew Bible, reflecting the Priestly source of the Pentateuch and the writings of the chronicler. Certainly the Hellenistic culture also played a role in the formation of the Septuagint.

The Septuagint was used extensively in the Jewish synagogues of the diaspora. Apparently, among these communities, material was accepted as part of the tradition which was not so regarded by those who preserved the Hebrew Bible. As a result, the contents of the Septuagint varied from that of the Hebrew Bible. We shall discuss this material later. Also the text used by the translators is one representing an earlier stage of development from that which is the Hebrew Bible in use today by the Jewish community. Thus, in this period, as the second century wanes, we see a divergence in the biblical tradition that will hold great importance for the future.

5. Esther

SUGGESTED READING: THE BOOK OF ESTHER, CHAPTERS 2, 3, 6 AND 9

As with the book of Daniel, which will be discussed next, Esther might be best described as a work of historical fiction. Many of the characters are historical, as are the settings. For instance, the "great King Ahasuerus" (A:1) is the Persian ruler Xerxes I, who reigned from 485 to 464 B.C. However, the events related and some of the protagonists are imaginary. The purpose of the unknown author was not to deceive but to use this literary form in order to encourage his readers during times of trial—times when the resolve to follow their religion was being tested by a foreign power hostile to Judaism.

The heroine and her uncle Mordecai, faithful Jews, defeat their enemy, Haman, and save the Jewish people, an event still memorialized by the feast of Purim. Some form of the story was written in Hebrew as early as the fourth century, and apparently several versions existed subsequently. During the second century B.C., a Greek translation was made. The story would certainly have had appeal to the oppressed Jews of the time. The version preserved in the Hebrew Bible is shorter than the one found in the Septuagint.

6. Daniel

SUGGESTED READING: THE BOOK OF DANIEL, CHAPTERS 1, 2, 3:1–23, 5, AND 13

With the attempt of Antiochus IV to impose Hellenistic culture on the Jews of Judea and his desecration of the temple in Jerusalem, the Maccabean revolt broke out. This must have certainly been a time of great stress for the Jews. It must have made clear the threat that faced them and the necessity to respond forcefully. Their heritage, their religious traditions, their very existence as a people were at stake. The book of Daniel was written to encourage the people of the Bible in this struggle. The date of composition is c. 166 B.C.

The author has taken his protagonist from earlier Jewish tradition and placed him in the period when Babylon was the threat (between the seventh and sixth centuries B.C.). The hero of the story remains faithful to the law and to the customs of Israel and is ultimately rescued by God. Like Esther this work is best described as historical fiction; the names and places are real but the events are imaginary. In telling the story of Daniel, the author wishes to encourage his countrymen and co-religionists to similarly remain true to their heritage.

Daniel is unique in several ways. For one, it was written originally in Hebrew, Aramaic and Greek. The last section (chapters 13-14) is not found in the Hebrew Bible of today, but is found in the Septuagint. Also, in the Septuagint, Daniel is placed among the prophets, whereas in the Hebrew Bible it is part of the section called the Writings.

7. The Apocalyptic Literary Form

The book of Daniel is also an example of a type of literary form that will become increasingly popular in coming centuries, apocalyptic. We have already seen its beginnings in the prophetic books of Isaiah, Ezekiel, Deutero-Isaiah and Zechariah. The prophets, however, focused upon Israel, God's people, and the future of the Davidic rule. The later apocalyptic writers had a far broader canvas; it was the universe itself. The struggle was cosmic; darkness and light were the primal forces. The symbolism is more elaborate and frequently difficult to divine. Finally, the prophets, though at times mysterious, really strive for clarity and are pragmatic. Their

concerns are usually immediate and the evils they challenge quite
concrete. On the other hand, obscurity is the stock in trade of the
apocalyptic authors; their aims are often mysterious. It is common
for later generations to see in these writings an explanation for
contemporary events, even up to the present day.

The visions found in Daniel, chapters 7–12, are apt examples
of this literary form. Found in them is a passage that will have
particular influence in the future. "I saw one like a human being
coming with the clouds of heaven. . . . To him was given dominion
and glory and kingship, that all peoples, nations, and languages
should serve him. His dominion is an everlasting dominion that
shall not pass away, and his kingship is one that shall never be
destroyed" (7:13–14).

What had happened to the people of the Bible to give rise to
apocalyptic literature such as Daniel? For one thing, their world
had changed. It now was vast compared to previous centuries.
Enormous forces were in play, especially when the power of Rome
began to emerge from the west. Antiochus IV had actually been
held as a hostage by the Romans. If God were to influence such a
world and come to the aid of his people, it could only be on a
cosmic scale. Apocalyptic literature sought to reassure the reader in
these times of chaos. The outcome was determined; even the coming of the day of the Lord was fixed. What was demanded of the
people by the apocalyptic author was the decision to remain faithful in the time of trial. It is easy to see the influence of this literature
on Jesus of Nazareth and his followers.

8. The Deuterocanonicals

By the middle of the second century B.C., with the inclusion of
Esther and Daniel, what was ultimately to be the Hebrew Bible was
complete. However, as mentioned earlier, additional material is
found in the Septuagint. Later, it would be the Septuagint that
would be accepted by the early Christian communities. These addi-

tional books are referred to as the Deuterocanonicals, i.e., those of the "second canon"—"canon," from the Greek meaning "reed," refers to "norm" or "rule." In biblical terms, a "canon" is a list of books officially approved and accepted by whatever religious body is concerned. Thus there is a "canon" accepted by the Jews which is the Hebrew Bible. Currently the Catholic community accepts the collection of books found in the Septuagint as "canonical." The Protestant communities accept as sacred scripture only those books found in the Hebrew Bible. The material that is referred to as deuterocanonical by Catholics is called by the Protestants the "Apocrypha."

a. Sirach

SUGGESTED READING: THE BOOK OF SIRACH, CHAPTERS 1–4

As is unusual for a biblical work, we know the author of Sirach, one Yeshua ben Eleazar ben Sira. His work, among the longest found in the Bible, is modeled after Proverbs, and is a rich collection of Israelite wisdom literature. The author was himself a student of Jewish tradition and a teacher living in Jerusalem between the third and second centuries B.C. Ben Sira wrote Sirach around 180 B.C. in Hebrew. As the Foreword tells us, his grandson translated the book into Greek c. 132 B.C. The original Hebrew version was known of in later years but was not included in the Hebrew Bible. The book is further evidence of the Jewish community's interest in a practical guide to living wisely, an interest we saw earlier in the case of Proverbs and Ecclesiastes.

b. Baruch

SUGGESTED READING: THE BOOK OF BARUCH, CHAPTERS 1–3:9, AND 6

As with Sirach, Baruch was originally written in Hebrew but only a Greek translation now exists. The attribution to the companion of Jeremiah is by later authors writing between the second and first centuries B.C. By recalling the dark days before and during the exile, Baruch reminds the reader that God once before restored his people and assures them that he will do so again. The Jews of the diaspora who hoped for such a restoration of the glory of the past would have responded positively to such a promise. "Look to the east, O Jerusalem, and see the joy that is coming to you from God. Look, your children are coming whom you sent away; they are coming, gathered from east and west at the word of the Holy One" (4:36–37).

c. Tobit

SUGGESTED READING: THE BOOK OF TOBIT, CHAPTERS 1, 2, AND 12

The original language of Tobit, written in the early part of the second century B.C., is debated. Except for fragments in Hebrew, only the Greek version has survived as part of the Septuagint. The work is a "romantic novel" set in the time of the destruction of the northern kingdom. The Jews of the tale are "strangers in a strange land" who survive under difficult conditions. The purpose of Tobit, however, is not simply to entertain. The reader is encouraged to live a pious life, faithful to God, and in doing so he will be assured of reward.

d. Judith

SUGGESTED READING: THE BOOK OF JUDITH, CHAPTERS 7–15

This work is similar to Tobit in that it is fictional. Set in the time of Nebuchadnezzar, Judith most likely dated from the early first century B.C. As no trace of a Hebrew version exists, the original language must have been Greek. The heroine, a far more dynamic and ruthless figure than Esther, is unique in biblical literature.

Of interest is the way God is portrayed in Judith as the one, true and transcendent divinity who created and rules the universe. He is the champion of the weak and is merciful to those who are faithful to him—again, a vision that would be of particular meaning to those Jews constantly struggling against the blandishments of a pagan culture.

e. 1 and 2 Maccabees

SUGGESTED READING: THE BOOKS OF 1 MACCABEES, CHAPTERS 1–4, AND 2 MACCABEES, CHAPTERS 6, 7, 9 AND 15

These two volumes give us an insight into struggle that must have been taking place among the Jews as the second century B.C. was coming to an end. The Hasmoneans ruled in Judea, but the majority of Jews were part of the diaspora with a particularly influential group living in Egypt. The Jews of the diaspora lived more intimately with the Hellenistic culture and were the most likely to have made an accommodation with it. The Jews of Palestine, on the other hand, were the more resistant to the inroads of Hellenism. 1 and 2 Maccabees typify these two contrasting responses.

1 Maccabees was written in Hebrew by an unknown author at the beginning of the first century B.C. As the work was not ultimately accepted by the Jewish community, only the Greek translation now exists. The book chronicles events from the beginning of the reign of Antiochus IV in 175 B.C. to the ascendancy of John Hyrcanus as the Hasmonean ruler of Judea in 134 B.C. 1 Maccabees defends the legitimacy of the Hasmonean dynasty.

2 Maccabees was written in Greek, though the author was a Jew from Alexandria, Egypt and he states that his work is a condensation of an original five volume work by Jason of Cyrene (2:19ff).

It covers Jewish history from 180 to 160 B.C. and was composed about twenty years earlier than 1 Maccabees and with a different purpose.

The author of 1 Maccabees praises those who revolted against the imposition of Hellenism and judges severely any Jew who compromised with the oppressor. The Maccabean revolutionaries are praised and the Hasmoneans legitimated by their violent rejection of the pagan culture. "They rescued the law out of the hands of the Gentiles and kings, and they never let the sinner gain the upper hand" (2:48).

2 Maccabees glorifies the role of the martyrs whose sufferings are described in detail. The author notes that some died because "their piety kept them from defending themselves, in view of their regard for that most holy day [the sabbath]" (6:11). These are as much the heroes of the work as are the revolutionaries in 1 Maccabees. It is this passive resistance that merits God's assistance.

Comparing 1 and 2 Maccabees, one notes how differently the deity is treated. For 1 Maccabees, God is never mentioned by name. He is completely transcendent and remote. The focus is on the human drama and there is no miraculous intervention by the divine. In 2 Maccabees, Yahweh is very much a "player," entering the action at crucial moments. "When the battle became fierce, there appeared to the enemy five resplendent men on horses with golden bridles, and they were leading the Jews" (10:29).

Both volumes see in the struggle of the Maccabeans a contest for the survival of Judaism versus an absorption into Hellenism. However, the author of 2 Maccabees not only wrote in Greek, he employed a rhetorical style of writing common in Hellenism. He is not the objective observer but a forceful partisan in relating the events he covers. Thus in opposing Hellenism he reveals its pervasive influence on the Jews of his time.

2 Maccabees contains unique elements that will have great influence in the future development of Judaism. These are the conviction of an afterlife and of a resurrection of the body. A martyr cries out, "You dismiss us from this present life, but the King of

the universe will raise us up to an everlasting renewal of life" (7:9). Even clearer is the author's observation, "In doing this [offering a sacrifice of expiation for the sins of fallen soldiers] [Judas] acted very well, taking account of the resurrection. For if he were not expecting that those who had fallen would rise again, it would have been superfluous and foolish to pray for the dead" (12:43–44). As we shall see, in a hundred years, Judaism will be sharply divided on the resurrection of the dead.

f. Wisdom

SUGGESTED READING: THE BOOK OF WISDOM, CHAPTERS 1, 2, 9 AND 10

The Septuagint gives the title of this book as "The Wisdom of Solomon." However, this attribution is a literary device to give prestige to the work of an unknown author writing about midway in the first century B.C. Thus Wisdom is the last of the biblical literature found in the Septuagint. Most likely another Alexandrian Jew, the author seeks to encourage his fellow members of the diaspora to remain faithful to their traditions. The temptation to conform to the dominant Hellenistic culture with its materialism and hedonism must have been intense. Given the fierce attack on idolatry in chapters 13 through 15 in Wisdom we can assume that these practices must have been particularly attractive. Also, the author wishes to comfort those who, because they have remained true to their heritage, are suffering persecution.

Yet, in spite of its anti-Hellenist bent, Wisdom is the most Hellenized book to be found in the Bible. It is originally in Greek (thus it is not found in the Hebrew Bible) and employs a didactic style frequently used in Greek philosophical writings. The author has some familiarity with such literature. The Hellenism of Wisdom should not be overstated. The poetry is characteristically Hebrew and the origin of death with the devil (2:24) is definitely not a Greek notion.

One concern of Wisdom, life after death, shows how the author was able to incorporate a Greek notion into traditional Hebrew thought. In the latter view, the only continued existence was some sort of shadow-like survival in a place for the dead ("sheol" in Hebrew and "hades" in Greek). Virtue was to be rewarded in this life, not in the next. We have already seen, particularly in Job, that there were problems with this view.

One solution was the idea of a "resurrection," at least of the just as we saw above in 2 Maccabees. Suggestions of such a possibility are found earlier. We read in Isaiah: "Your dead shall live, their corpses shall rise . . ." (26:19). For whatever reason, Wisdom does not mention this possibility but turns to the platonic concepts of body and soul where the spiritual element is limited by the material: "For a perishable body weighs down the soul and this earthly tent burdens the thoughtful mind" (9:15).

The reward of a good life is the immortality of one's soul. "Giving heed to [Wisdom's] laws is the assurance of immortality, and immortality brings one near to God" (6:18–19). Wisdom has skillfully blended the anthropocentric Greek approach with the theocentrism of the Hebrew. The ethical is linked with an eternal reward.

STUDY QUESTIONS

1. What challenges faced the Jews in Judea when Antiochus IV took power?
2. What circumstances does the book of Ecclesiastes reflect?
3. How did the use of Aramaic and Greek affect the biblical traditions?
4. What is the "Septuagint"?
5. What is the literary form of the book of Esther?
6. In what way does the book of Daniel resemble that of Esther?
7. What are the characteristics of the "apocalyptic" literary form? What are examples of its use?

8. Where are the deuterocanonicals found? The apocrypha?
9. What interest does the book of Sirach reflect?
10. What hope is expressed in Baruch?
11. In what way do the books of Tobit and Judith resemble each other?
12. What events are covered by 1 and 2 Maccabees? How does the second volume differ from the first?
13. What does the book of Wisdom encourage the Jews of the disaspora to do?

Transition

The story of the people of the Bible did not end here. They are with us still. However, the Bible in both its Hebrew and Greek forms is complete, though variations and other translations existed, as they still do. But we have reached a period of transition. From the Christian perspective, the crucial point is reflected in the way we have dated the preceding and succeeding material. To see things as B.C. (Before Christ) or A.D. (Anno Domini, Year of Our Lord) is a view not shared by the people of the Bible. A crucial transition for them does lie ahead, but it is not the advent of Jesus of Nazareth. In 70 A.D. Jerusalem and its great temple will be destroyed, radically changing the picture of the Jewish religion. However, neither of these events was at "center stage." That spot was occupied by Rome and the greatest of the Caesars, Augustus, who had brought peace to the largest empire the world had known.

From the perspective of history, it was not Augustus who would shape the future. Rather it was a Jewish child, born in upper Galilee, known as Jesus of Nazareth. What we know of him is found in the works which make up the New Testament. To these we now turn.

Part Two
THE NEW TESTAMENT

THE CHRONOLOGY OF THE NEW TESTAMENT DOCUMENTS ARRANGED ACCORDING TO THE RELATED COMMUNITIES

DATE	PAULINE	ROME	ANTIOCH	JOHANNINE	OTHERS[4]
APOSTOLIC AGE (33–66 A.D.)	1 and 2 Thessalonians Galatians Philippians 1 and 2 Corinthians Philemon	Romans	Galatians[2]		
SUB-APOSTOLIC AGE (66–100 A.D.)	1 and 2 Timothy Titus Colossians[1] Ephesians Luke Acts	Mark[3] 1 Peter Hebrews	Acts[2] Matthew	John 1, 2 and 3 John	James 2 Peter Jude Revelation

(1) Colossians' authorship is in question. If it is by Paul himself, then it would have to be dated in the apostolic age.
(2) These documents contain information about communities other than the ones from which they originated.
(3) The exact place from which Mark originated is disputed. However, a relationship to the community in Rome is not impossible.
(4) These documents are unrelated to any specific community.

86

I

Introduction: The Beginning of the Christian Era

- The Birth of Jesus of Nazareth (c. 5 B.C.1)
- The Death of Herod the Great (4 B.C.)
- Judea Becomes a Roman Province (6 A.D.)
- Tiberius Succeeds Augustus as Emperor (14 A.D.)
- Ovid, the Roman Poet, Dies (18 A.D.)
- Death of Jesus of Nazareth (c. 30 A.D.)
- Caligula Becomes Emperor (37 A.D.)
- Caligula Is Assassinated and Claudius Becomes Emperor (42 A.D.)
- The Romans Invade Britain (43 A.D.)
- Paul of Tarsus Sets Out on His First Missionary Journey (45 A.D.)
- Claudius Poisoned and Nero Becomes Emperor (54 A.D.)
- The First Recorded Persecution of Christians Under Nero and the Traditional Death of Peter and Paul (c. 64 A.D.)
- Nero Commits Suicide (68 A.D.) and He Is Eventually Succeeded by Vespasian (69 A.D.)
- The Jewish Revolt and the Razing of Jerusalem and Destruction of the Temple (70 A.D.) by Titus, Emperor (79–81 A.D.)
- Trajan, Emperor (98–116 A.D.), Under Whom the Roman Empire Reaches Its Greatest Geographical Extent

SUGGESTED READING: ACTS 1:1–2:47

A. THE OLD AND THE NEW

As we have seen how the documents which made up the Hebrew Bible flowed from the experiences of a particular people over almost two millennia. Their glories, triumphs, defeats and sufferings all found their expression in the marvelous series of books that make up the Hebrew Bible. We saw how later experiences and later events modified earlier traditions and how documents would be edited and reedited to reflect what happened in subsequent generations. In some cases, books were attributed to figures long dead at the time of their writing, the prestige of the earlier figure being used to enhance the work of an anonymous author. There will be similar processes at work as we come now to the New Testament.

But there will also be striking differences, one of which is the time scale. Between the appearance of the New Testament's first document and its final one, only about fifty or sixty years will have elapsed, not almost two thousand. Also, whereas the Hebrew Bible arose from the religious experience of a more or less single ethnic group, the sources of the New Testament were communities, often made up of various nationalities. We can get some feeling of this variety from that first Pentecost as described in Acts (The Acts of the Apostles). Peter's audience included "Parthians, Medes, Elamites, and residents of Mesopotamia, Judea and Cappadocia, Pontus and Asia, Phrygia and Pamphylia, Egypt and the parts of Libya belonging to Cyrene, and visitors from Rome . . . Cretans and Arabs" (2:9–11). These were Jews or Jewish converts, but we can be sure that the earliest Christian communities were equally diverse, both ethnically and linguistically.

Even though the development of the New Testament was over a much shorter period of time, the pattern will be similar to that of the Hebrew Bible. The methods of "historical criticism," mentioned earlier, can also be applied to the documents of the Christian Testament. Knowing the author, editors, time and place of composition, purpose, and the literary form will help us gain some understanding of the communities that lay behind the formation of the New Testament.

B. THE HISTORICAL CONTEXT OF THE NEW TESTAMENT

As with the Hebrew Bible, the history of the period in question is also central to our understanding of the origins of the New Testament. For our purpose two groups are significant: the Romans and the Jews. As we closed our previous section the most important figures in each of these histories were just making their appearances on the world's stage.

1. The Romans

The independence of Israel ended in 63 B.C. with the conquest of Palestine by the Roman general Pompey. Later Pompey would be defeated by his rival, Julius Caesar. In the power struggle following the latter's assassination, it was Caesar's nephew, Octavian, who emerged triumphant. Taking the name Augustus, the new emperor was successful in establishing a modicum of peace in the empire during his reign from 30 B.C. to 14 A.D. The Augustine line ruled until the suicide of Nero in 68 A.D., and for the balance of the century a series of military leaders succeeded as emperors.

The Roman genius for organization and bureaucracy provided an important element in the historical development of Christianity. By imposing a rule of law, completing a vast system of protected roads and seaways, and the staffing of the empire with representatives of the central administration, the Romans had made communication and travel both safe and efficient. Added to this was the *lingua franca* of the empire, Greek. Whatever might be the local language, the stranger who spoke Greek could always find an audience. These factors were essential to the rapid spread of the new religion.

2. The Jews

The new religion began as part of the old. Thus Christianity's early history was intertwined with that of the Jewish people. The vast majority of Jews lived outside of Palestine, concentrated mostly in the urban centers of the empire. Their religious and social lives centered around the synagogues. These, in turn, reflected the divisions of Judaism which we will discuss shortly. The Jews lived in a somewhat uneasy peace with their Gentile neighbors, being occasionally subjected to persecution. However, they were not without their converts and sympathizers in the non-Jewish community. But, being strictly monotheistic, it was impossible for the pious Jew to participate in the pagan rituals sometimes required by the authorities. Most of the time, however, the Jews enjoyed certain exemptions from these demands.

For most pious Jews, the focus of their religion was the great temple in Jerusalem. A prominent exception to this was the Essenes whom we will discuss below. Also, the majority of the diaspora looked to the homeland as the hope for their nationalistic aspirations. The message of the Hebrew Bible, with its promises of an ultimate restoration of Israel's glory, had not been lost on the succeeding generations. Events in Palestine would always resonate in the Jewish communities throughout the empire.

Since Pompey's conquest, Palestine was ruled by a series of petty potentates, governors and procurators. It was occupied territory under military control. In Jerusalem, the temple's high priest was recognized as having considerable local influence, but he served at the pleasure of his Roman masters. However, having had the good fortune to be on the winning side of a dynastic struggle, Herod the Great (37–4 B.C.) exercised considerable authority during his reign. He did much to bring prestige back to the holy city, and it was he who began the final restoration of its great temple of Jerusalem. He also contributed much of the Hellenization of Palestine. Nevertheless, ruling as he did with an iron hand, Herod died unmourned by his people.

Herod's kingdom was divided among his heirs, but in 6 A.D. Judea and the surrounding territory became a Roman province under the control of a procurator or military governor. One of these was Pontius Pilate (26–36 A.D.) who was eventually removed from office for abuses of power. Considering the normal tyrannies of such rulers, we have here eloquent testimony to the extremes to which Pilate must have gone. Local rule was reestablished in Judea with Herod Agrippa (37–44 A.D.), and after him the area again became a Roman province.

Palestine was also a very volatile province. Revolt continually boiled just below the surface. In 66 A.D. the Jewish wars began with open revolution. Nero dispatched Vespasian and his legions to put it down. But as Vespasian marched toward Jerusalem he was declared emperor, and he left his son Titus to continue the campaign to its victorious conclusion. Though it was not the intention of Titus, the conquest of Jerusalem resulted in the destruction of the great temple. In 70 A.D. the city itself was razed and much of its surviving populace was led off into slavery. Titus then succeeded his father as emperor. An arch, still extant in the Roman Forum, memorializes his victory. One panel on the arch shows the treasures of the temple being carried away by the conqueror. As we shall see, this tragic event will be a watershed in both Jewish and Christian history.

3. Jewish Religious Groups

From the New Testament, we are familiar with some of the Jewish groups present among the population of Palestine and in the diaspora. Knowledge of these groups is important to our under-standing of the events that surround the rise of Christianity.

a. Sadducees

The origin of their name is obscure. They emerged during the era of Persian domination and were a religious party made up of the priestly aristocracy. Their influence stemmed from the role of the high priesthood of the temple in Jewish affairs. By collaborating with the rule of Rome, they maintained their position in Jewish life. Religious as well as political conservatives, the Sadducees recognized as authoritative only the torah and rejected any non-biblical tradition. In contrast to their chief rivals, the Pharisees, they rejected the notion of a resurrection of the dead and the existence of angels and spirits. The Sadducees, as a group, did not survive the disaster of 70 A.D.

b. Pharisees

Their name means the "separated" and reflects their determination to live an unsullied, pious life as faithful Jews. They made their appearance around 140 B.C. and focused their lives on the law, rigidly interpreted and observed. However, the Pharisees recognized non-biblical commentaries on the torah, and it was this that gave them sufficient flexibility to be regarded by their opponents as "liberals." Predominantly a group of laymen, their number included some members of priesthood.

As their lifestyle required a certain level of income, the Pharisees were what we would call "middle class." Their goal was a holy nation, a theocracy, and they opposed nationalistic aspirations in a secular sense. Tending to "go along" with the current circumstances of Roman rule, the Pharisees pursued a realistic policy. Though they held to a resurrection of the dead, they focused their concern in living a pious life in the present. Contrasting themselves to the "rabble who know not the law," the Pharisees probably deserved their reputation for being haughty and "holier than thou."

c. Essenes

In 1947 two Arab shepherds, exploring a cave near Palestine's Dead Sea, came upon a collection ancient scrolls stored in jars. These turned out to be the library of a Jewish religious sect who had built a monastery-like complex at a site not far away called Qumran. With this discovery, scholars had their first extensive insight into a group called the Essenes or "pious ones." The Essenes originated during the reign of the Maccabees in 150 B.C., separating from mainstream Judaism in a dispute over the high priesthood. The sect disappeared around 70 A.D. in the tragic events of the Jewish wars.

Isolated from Jewish life and scorning any participation in the rituals of the Jerusalem temple, as mentioned, the Essenes played little or no role in the early years of Christianity and are not mentioned in the New Testament. However, there are resemblances between Essene organization and beliefs which may have influenced Christianity. Such possibilities will be discussed later on.

d. Zealots

These were, as their name might imply, fanatical nationalists, inspired by the Hebrew Bible promises of a restored kingdom, interpreted in largely political terms. Among the Zealots were terrorists who used assassination to forward their cause. The Romans dubbed these "sicarii," "stabbers," reflecting their practice of knifing their victims. Some of these extremists instigated the revolt that began the Jewish wars. By forcing out anyone of moderate opinion, the Zealots brought on the ultimate tragedy of 70 A.D.

e. Scribes

These were not a separate religious group as such. Trained in the law and its interpretations, the scribes were the intellectuals of their society and exercised leadership roles in the synagogues of Palestine and throughout the diaspora. A prestigious group, most of the scribes were Pharisees—hence the tendency of the gospels to link the two groups.

4. After 70 A.D.

As was noted, the Sadducees disappeared along with their power base, the temple in Jerusalem. The Essene monastery at Qumran was destroyed as Titus moved toward Jerusalem. Survivors joined other Jews who held out at Masada until the fortress was overrun and destroyed by the Romans. The exact fate of other Essenes is unknown, though groups of "pious" Jews, known as the "Hasidim," reappear in Jewish history, with no connection, however, to this earlier group. The Zealots remained active, creating unrest until their final defeat in the second century A.D.

We know that some of the Pharisaic sect also joined the Christian communities. Paul of Tarsus, of whom we shall see more, was hardly an exception. The influence of the Pharisees on Christianity is hard to measure but should not be underestimated either. However, the great contributions of the Pharisees lay in Judaism itself. They made possible the survival of the religion and the culture after the destruction of the holy city and the great temple which had been the very heart of Judaism. The achievement of the Pharisees stands beside that of those who saved the Jewish heritage following the disaster of 587 B.C. The Jewish religion today rests upon the accomplishments of these first century Pharisees.

Unfortunately, there was a tragic consequence to their achievement. In order to preserve their religious heritage, the Pharisaic leaders of the synagogues expelled those they regarded as deviating from their traditions. Among those who suffered in these excommunications were many Jewish Christians. The resulting pain, suffering and even loss of life gave rise to the hostility toward the Pharisees and their scribes we find in the gospels. Later, it will be directed simply toward the "Jews" as a group. Here we find some of the roots of the antisemitism which will mar Christianity in later centuries. In fairness, however, some of this nascent antisemitism came from the Gentile world, especially in the years following the Jewish wars.

The stage is now set for the beginnings of Christianity.

STUDY QUESTIONS

1. What were the contributions of the Roman empire to the spread of Christianity?
2. What were the principal Jewish religious groups at the time of Jesus and what were their distinctive features?
3. What happened to Judaism after 70 A.D.?

II

Paul of Tarsus

A. THE BEGINNINGS

SUGGESTED READING: ACTS 9:1-3

"Thus at the outset we come up against that fundamental condition to which experience is subject, by virtue of which the beginnings of all things tend to be materially out of our grasp." (Pierre Teilhard de Chardin, *The Phenomenon of Man* [New York: Harper Torchbooks, 1961], p. 90).

What Teilhard found true about the origins of life, we find valid in our attempts to recover some knowledge of the first manifestations of Christianity. As in evolution where later forms of life obliterated the earlier, the later Christian communities have obscured any definitive grasp of their predecessors. We can make assumptions, of course. Obviously, some of those who knew Jesus of Nazareth and had direct knowledge of his life and words came together and, in this primordial gathering, experienced his resurrected presence in their midst. In time they sought to share their memories and their conviction of Jesus' resurrection with others, now convinced that Jesus of Nazareth was the expected "messiah."

As we saw in Part One, "messiah" (Greek, "Christos"), meaning "anointed one," is the Hebrew Bible's designation for the kings of Israel, stemming from the manner of indicating their religious character as sacred. The exilic and post-exilic prophets expressed the hope for a restoration of the Davidic monarchy and a return to the glories of the past. However, during the intertestamental period, this expectation was secularized into the hope for a Jewish empire established by Yahweh's intervention. For some, the kingdom of God would be inaugurated by the appearance of a "messiah" who would lead Israel to victory. For others, however, the title had only a religious meaning. The "anointed one" was an "apocalyptic" figure who would herald the end of the age. Jesus of Nazareth, if he used the title at all, employed it in this latter sense.

The first disciples of Jesus sought first to spread his message among their Jewish co-religionists who shared their messianic expectations. As converts were welcomed into their midst, small communities would have been formed. The movement began in the Jerusalem area and then among the Jews of nearby urban centers. Just how soon they became identified as a definite group or sect within Judaism we cannot tell, but it was not long before they were actually called "Messianists," "Christians" in the Greek, stemming from this central conviction that Jesus of Nazareth was the long-awaited messiah.

However, it will not be until almost a generation has passed that we have direct information about these Christian communities. "I suggest, therefore, that the term 'Apostolic Age' should be confined to that second one-third of the first century, and that *the last one-third of the century should be designated as the 'Subapostolic Period.'* (Author's emphasis) With the exception of the undisputed letters of Paul, most of the New Testament would have been written in this last one-third of the century . . ." (R.E. Brown, *The Churches the Apostles Left Behind,* p. 15). Thus, the first direct evidence we have of the Christian communities is found in the letters of Paul of Tarsus.

B. PAUL OF TARSUS

SUGGESTED READING: ACTS 7:54–8:3

Paul's letters tell us much about the personality and thought of the man, but only occasionally do they give us biographical data, Galatians being the most extensive. However, the New Testament's Acts of the Apostles (Acts) gives us a more detailed record. But this document was composed as much as twenty years after Paul's death, its purpose was not strictly biographical, and the author had mostly indirect knowledge of "the apostle." In spite of these limitations Acts can be accepted as a source for our brief account of Paul's most remarkable life.

1. His Roots

Having two names, Saul and Paul, one Jewish and the other Greek, indicates his dual heritage. In the early years of the first century, Paul was born in the imperial town of Tarsus, the capital of the province of Cilicia, in the south of present-day Turkey. It was a cultural center noted for its educational institutions, and the young Paul appears to have taken advantage of them since his writings give evidence of training in the Greek classics. A "Hellenized" Jew by education and upbringing, he wrote in Greek and made use of the Septuagint, the Greek translation of the Hebrew Bible. Paul also was a citizen of Rome, something that proved to be advantageous during his later career.

However Paul was also a Jew, speaking Aramaic and reading Hebrew. A Pharisee, he trained in Jerusalem under one of the leading rabbis of that day, Gamaliel. Destined certainly to be a rabbi himself, Paul must have appeared to his contemporaries as a person of great promise. When first seen in Acts, it is at the assassination of Stephen (7:5) where he is depicted as one of the perpetrators. He then participated in a persecution of Jesus' followers in Jerusalem and, at his own request, was sent to Damascus to continue a similar persecution in that city (9:1-2).

2. The Conversion

SUGGESTED READING: ACTS 9:1-30; 22:1-16; 26:4-18

As he is about to enter Damascus, Paul undergoes a dramatic conversion which he describes in detail (22:3-16, 26:2-18) and refers to in his letter to the Galatians (1:12). Convinced that Jesus of Nazareth is the risen messiah, the Christ, Paul enters upon a period of meditation. After a year spent in Arabia (Nabatea) Paul returns to Damascus for three years and then goes to his home town of Tarsus. In 44 A.D., Barnabas, a leader of the Christian community, comes to bring Paul to Antioch.

3. The First Missionary Journey

SUGGESTED READING: ACTS 13:1–14:28

A more detailed treatment of the important early Christian community in Antioch will come later. For the present, we only note that the Syrian city became the base for Paul's subsequent missionary journeys. On the first of these, beginning in 46 A.D., Paul traveled to Cyprus, then to the mainland of modern Turkey, going inland to the Roman provinces of Pamphylia, Pisidia, and Galatia. On arriving in a city, Paul would first seek to reach the Jewish community with his message that Jesus of Nazareth was the hoped-for messiah. When, as was frequently the case, he met with opposition, Paul would turn to the non-Jewish or Gentile population. Converts from this group and those Jews who had accepted Paul's message were formed into the local Christian community. It should be noted that while these early Christians gathered separately for their own religious meetings, many of their number still participated in the life of the Jewish community, attending the synagogues. Christianity would be regarded as a Jewish sect for another thirty years at least. It was Paul's custom to maintain a close relationship with the communities he founded, principally through his letters.

Paul returned overland to Antioch and reported on his successes, particularly with the Gentiles. Now arises the central controversy that was to prove so divisive between Paul and other church leaders, between Christians and Jews and among Christians themselves. Symbolic of the problem was the Jewish practice of circumcision. In the Hellenized world, much of daily social life centered on the great public baths, whose ruins are architectural wonders even today. Nudity was very common, and the popular athletic contests were also held in the nude. It is easy to see why circumcision held out little attraction for the non-Jew. Add to this the restrictive character of the Jewish laws governing diet and conduct, we can see how problems would arise in Paul's mixed communities of Jews and Gentiles.

4. The Controversy

SUGGESTED READING: ACTS 15:1–35; GALATIANS 2:1–14

The more conservative Christians, who were likely to have been converts from among the Pharisaic Jews, insisted that compliance with the Jewish law was required of all Christians, Jew and Gentile alike, as we see described in Acts (15:5). Paul understandably wished to free his missionary activity from such a serious limitation. A meeting was held in Jerusalem (15:1ff), attended by Paul and Barnabas, where actually Peter defended the position taken by Paul and where James, acting as head of the Jerusalem community, rendered the decision: Gentile converts are not required to submit to circumcision but are simply to "abstain from what has been sacrificed to idols and from blood and from what is strangled and from fornication" (15:29). Unfortunately this decision did not settle the problem. In fact, Paul, in writing in his letter to the Galatians (2:1–14), seems unaware of the meeting's conclusion and is involved in a dispute with Peter on the very subject of relations with Gentiles. It seems reasonable then to conclude that this controversy continued to create problems until the Gentiles came to predominate in the Christian communities and relationship between them and the Jewish community ended.

5. The Second Missionary Journey

SUGGESTED READING: ACTS 15:36–18:22

In 49 A.D. Paul set out on his second missionary journey. This time he traveled overland to the province of Galatia, crossing to its west coast at Troas. He sailed the Aegean to Philippi which brought him into Europe for the first time. Paul went north into Macedonia and visited Thessalonica and then journeyed south to the cultural center of the empire, Athens. Though given a hearing in the Areopagus, the main forum of the city, Paul failed to impress his hearers and he continued south to one of ancient world's crossroads, Corinth. There his reception was much different and he founded a thriving Christian community, strongly Gentile in character. It was in Corinth, in 51 A.D., that Paul wrote the first of his extant letters, 1 and 2 Thessalonians. These are the oldest documents in the New Testament. Later in that year Paul recrossed the Aegean to Ephesus. However, his visit to this most important political and cultural center was brief, and Paul sailed for the coast of Palestine. After paying a short visit to the Christian community in Jerusalem, Paul then returned to his base at Antioch. His stay there was lengthy, over eighteen months.

6. The Third Missionary Journey

SUGGESTED READING: ACTS 19:1–21:14

In the spring of 54 A.D. Paul began his most significant journey. It took him back to the area of Galatia he had visited before and then on to Ephesus, the center of his activity for the next three years. Part of the time Paul was imprisoned—most likely for disturbing the peace, from his cell Paul wrote his letters to the Galatians and the Philippians. Also, while he was in Ephesus, word reached Paul of serious conflicts among the members of the Christian community in Corinth. He dispatched two letters in response to these reports. The first no longer exists; the second is now known as 1 Corinthians. Paul followed these up with a personal visit and another letter, also not in existence. The troubles remained unresolved, and later Paul sent his associate Titus to make another attempt to assauge the situation.

But now there was trouble in Ephesus. Local merchants had done a thriving business selling statuettes of the local deity, Artemis, a goddess of fertility, symbolically bedecked with numerous *scrota*. The emergence of Christianity was seen as a threat to this commerce and rioting ensued. It was judged politic for Paul to leave town, so he set off for Macedonia and, after a report from Titus, wrote a fourth letter to the Corinthian community, our 2 Corinthians. In December of 57 A.D. Paul returned to that city and remained for three months. He planned to visit Rome and even to travel on to Spain. However, before making an appearance in the empire's capital city, Paul thought it advisable to introduce himself to this prestigious community of Christians. To this end, Paul composed his most profound work, the letter to the Romans, early in 58 A.D.

7. To Jerusalem and Rome

SUGGESTED READING: ACTS 19:1–21:14

First, however, Paul returned to Jerusalem, bringing with him a collection taken up for the poor of that city. He left Philippi and, after making several ports-of-call, reached the holy city in time to celebrate Pentecost. Whatever his hopes were, Paul's reception was not friendly. Apparently the local Christian community had still not been reconciled to Paul's liberal policy regarding the reception of Gentiles into his communities. This hostility, however, was as nothing compared to that which greeted Paul on his appearance in the precincts of the great temple. The crowds of Jews, gathered to celebrate the feast, rioted when they saw him. Threats of assassination made it wise for the local Roman commander, Claudius Lysias, to send Paul down to the coastal bastion of Caesarea Maritima where he remained imprisoned for two years.

When Paul was finally brought to trial, he "appealed to Caesar," invoking his right as a Roman citizen to be judged by an imperial court. This appeal was to send him under guard to Rome. The journey was a perilous one, necessitating a winter's stay on the island of Malta. On arriving in the capital city, Paul was placed under house arrest for two years, which had the advantage of giving him access to the Christians of area. At this time, he wrote the touching letter to Philemon. Most commentators agree that this was the last of Paul's authentic letters.

"He lived there two whole years at his own expense and welcomed all who came to him, proclaiming the kingdom of God and teaching about the Lord Jesus Christ with all boldness and without hindrance" (Acts 28:30–31). These closing words of the Acts of the Apostles are the final biblical record of Paul's activities. Many traditions exist about his later life. He would appear to have been executed sometime during the reign of the emperor Nero (64–68 A.D.). Due to the heritage of his letters preserved in the New Testament, Paul is second only to Jesus in his influence on Christianity.

C. THE PAULINE LETTERS

Paul's correspondence was copied and recopied, collected and circulated among the Christian communities in the years that followed the apostle's death. 2 Peter (3:15–16) appears to refer to such a collection of letters. Marcion, in 144 A.D., listed Paul's letters in this order: Galatians, 1 and 2 Corinthians, Romans, 1 and 2 Thessalonians, Ephesians, Colossians, Philippians, and Philemon. The omission of the two letters to Timothy and the one to Titus, known as the Pastorals, from this early list reinforces the general scholarly opinion that these letters are not authentically Pauline but were written by another hand and attributed to Paul. In addition, there is a similar opinion that Ephesians is not authentically Pauline. A majority of scholars make a similar judgment concerning Colossians.[2] We will take up the background to these conclusions later.

It should be clear, however, that all of these letters, authentic or not, were eventually accepted by the Christian churches as part of their sacred heritage to be zealously preserved for future generations, and they give us a precious insight into the Christian communities in the apostolic and sub-apostolic ages.

STUDY QUESTIONS

1. Describe the circumstances of Paul's conversion to Christ.
2. What was the central problem to face Paul on his missionary journeys?
3. How was this matter resolved?
4. What series of events brought Paul to Rome?

III

The Communities of the Apostolic Age: Thessalonica, Galatia, Philippi

A. THESSALONICA

SUGGESTED READINGS: ACTS 17:1–8, 1 AND 2 THESSALONIANS

1. Paul's Mission

On his second missionary journey Paul reached Troas on the coast of Asia Minor. There he received a vision (Acts 16:9–10) encouraging him to cross over into Macedonia. Paul did so and thus entered Europe for the first time.

After landing at Neapolis, he journeyed inland to Philippi and began to spread the message of Christ among his co-religionists in the Jewish community, but he quickly ran into trouble and was forced to move on. As we shall see later, he did manage to leave a Christian community behind him in Philippi. Traveling on, Paul reached Thessalonica in 49 or 50 A.D.

As we read in Acts, "Paul and Silas . . . came to Thessalonica, where there was a synagogue of the Jews. And Paul went in, as was his custom, and on three sabbath days argued with them from the scriptures" (17:1–2). Paul enjoyed an initial success by converting some Jews and a greater number of Gentiles. Then, probably due to his liberal policy of mixing Jews and Gentiles as well as his claim that Jesus was the messiah, Paul engendered the hostility of the Jewish community. A riot resulted which drove him out of town. Going south now, Paul arrived in Athens and, while there, he sent Timothy back to Thessalonica to check on things. Finally, from Corinth in 51 A.D., Paul wrote the first of his two letters to the Thessalonians. These are the earliest of the documents that ultimately went to form the New Testament.

2. The Meaning of "Church"

In four documents we refer to as "gospels," the word "church" is found only in Matthew and there only three times, leading to the conclusion that this was not a term used by Jesus himself, but came into use in the early days of Christianity. We find it first in the opening line of 1 Thessalonians: "Paul, Silvanus, and Timothy, to the church of the Thessalonians . . ." (1:1).

Our word "church" derives from an Anglo-Saxon word rooted in the Greek, "kyriakon," meaning "the Lord's (house)." The words for "church" in the Romance languages, i.e., "église," "iglesia" and "chiesa," reflect the Greek word "ekklesia" which was used in the Septuagint to translate the Hebrew "kahal." For the Greeks, "ekklesia" simply meant an assembly of people. Among the Jews, on the other hand, a "kahal" was specifically a religious assembly, as in "kahal Yahweh" (cf. Deut 23:2 and Jgs 20:2).

Paul's authentic letters use "church" in the Jewish sense when he refers to a local Christian community. Only later, particularly in Ephesians, will the term "church" be applied to the whole of Christianity itself. As Christians began to see themselves as distinct from the Jewish community, they took on the identity of the true "kahal Yahweh," the "gathering of God" or "church."

3. The Meaning of "Gospel"

"Gospel" comes to us from the Anglo-Saxon expression "good tidings," "good news" or "good word." It translates the Greek, "euangelion," which has the same meaning. Such is the word's meaning for Paul in 1 Thessalonians: "our message of the gospel came to you not in word only . . ." (1:5). The apostle reflects the Hebrew Bible usage, examples of which we find in Isaiah: "I give to Jerusalem a herald of good tidings. . . . How beautiful upon the mountains are the feet of the messenger who announces peace, who brings good news, who announces salvation, who says to Zion, 'Your God reigns. . . . The spirit of the Lord God is upon me, because the Lord has anointed me; he has sent me to bring good news to the oppressed, to bind up the brokenhearted, to proclaim liberty to the captives, and release to the prisoners' " (41:27; 52:7; 61:1).

The "gospel," the "good news," is for Paul the core of the Christian experience. The "gospel of Christ" (1 Thess 3:2) is what Christ himself is for the Christian rather than a message, oral or written, about Christ. Only later will "gospel" refer to a written document. Such a usage stems from the opening words of Mark, "The beginning of the good news of Jesus Christ, the Son of God" (1:1).

In the apostolic age, it appears that Pauline communities regarded themselves as "churches" formed around the preaching of the "gospel." As we now see in Paul's letters, a host of problems arise when it comes to the understanding and application of the "good news" in differing circumstances. The empire, with its rich mixture of ethnic groups, languages and cultures, resulted in an equal diversity among the Christian communities resulting in differing challenges.

4. The Challenge of Persecution

In 1 Thessalonians, Paul seeks to encourage the community he founded as it faces persecution from Jew and Gentile alike. In undergoing this, he tells them, "you, brothers and sisters, became imitators of the churches of God in Christ Jesus that are in Judea, for you suffered the same things from your own compatriots as they did from the Jews" (2:14). The hostility faced by these early Christians is understandable. Jews accepting Jesus as the messiah would be a source of distress for their unconverted family and friends, especially in their close-knit communities. It was also likely that Paul was accepting Gentiles into the local church without circumcision, a practice that would further have irritated the Jews.

Similarly, the conversion of a Gentile must also have been traumatic. Family, religious and other relationships played a central role in the civil life of that day. For a Gentile to join the Christian community meant severing these associations and isolating the person from the normal life of the city. Paul's communities did not have an easy time of it, something reflected in 1 and 2 Thessalonians.

5. The Parousia

One aspect of the "good news" must have profoundly affected the life of the Thessalonian Christians—the belief that one day quite soon Jesus would return in glory. In 1 Thessalonians Paul speaks of "the coming of our Lord Jesus with all his saints," and says that "the Lord himself, with a cry of command, with the archangel's call and with the sound of God's trumpet, will descend from heaven" (3:13; 4:16). Then in 2 Thessalonians he writes of "when the Lord Jesus is revealed from heaven with his mighty angels" (1:7). The Greek word, "parousia," meaning "arrival," is given to this expectation, and it is obvious from these letters and others of Paul that this return was thought to be in the near future.

One hint of how the community might have been influenced by the expectation of the parousia is found in Paul's admonition from 2 Thessalonians: "Anyone unwilling to work should not eat" (3:10). Some Christians, presuming that the end was near, apparently were abandoning their occupations and were just waiting for

Christ's return. However, it also appears that the Thessalonians were concerned about another aspect of the parousia.

Even though the Thessalonians had been Christian but a short time, some of their number must have died. In this period, neither the Jews nor the Gentiles had any clear notion of the fate that awaited one who had died. The possibility of annihilation was real —hence the concern that the Thessalonians had expressed to Paul. He responds in 1 Thessalonians: "But we do not want you to be uninformed, brothers and sisters, about those who have died, so that you may not grieve as others do who have no hope" (4:13). The apostle reassures his readers. "For since we believe that Jesus died and rose again, even so, through Jesus, God will bring with him those who have died . . . we who are alive, who are left until the coming of the Lord, will by no means precede those who have died" (4:15).

It should be noted that Paul does not doubt his own presence at the climactic event, so he can go on to say, "Then we who are alive, who are left, will be caught up in the clouds together with [those who have died] to meet the Lord in the air" (4:17). However, in dealing with the concern of the Thessalonians over their deceased co-religionists, Paul reinforced the conviction of some that the final day was soon to come. Even in the short time between the two letters written to them, there was a growing impatience with the delay, and Paul must warn the community in 2 Thessalonians: "As to the coming of our Lord Jesus Christ and our being gathered together to him, we beg you, brothers and sisters, not to be quickly shaken in mind or alarmed . . . to the effect that the day of the Lord is already here" (2:1-2). He goes on to explain (2:3ff) why the parousia has been delayed. As we shall see with time, the expectation of the final day will become more and more muted in the Pauline communities.

In this connection we should note that these early Christian communities were not isolated from one another, but in communication. "So that you [the Thessalonians] became an example to all the believers in Macedonia and in Achaia" (1:7). It is likely that Paul's letters were circulated among the communities he founded and eventually to others as well, in time becoming part of the New Testament when it took shape in the next century.

6. Summary

We see in these earliest letters of Paul a pattern that will become familiar. The apostle founds a community and keeps in touch with it through intermediaries or by personal visits. He preaches his understanding of the "good news of Christ Jesus." Subsequently, however, other Christians arrive with another interpretation of Jesus' message and questions arise concerning the correct meaning of the "gospel." Then the apostle learns of conduct at variance with his "gospel," and when unable to deal with the matter directly, Paul writes letters which correct, advise and admonish, all on his own authority as the one from whom the community first heard the "good news." Early on, Christians must have recognized what a treasure they had in these letters, first circulating them among other churches and eventually collecting them as part of the Christian tradition.

B. GALATIA

SUGGESTED READING: ACTS 14:1–13; GALATIANS

On each of his missionary journeys Paul went through the Roman province of Galatia, an area that lies on the Anatolian plain in the center of modern Turkey. He visited the towns of Iconium, Lystra and Derbe where we can assume he founded Christian communities. These churches of Galatia were very important to the apostle, as he was to them. We have clear evidence of this in the letter he wrote "to the churches of Galatia" (1:2) from Ephesus during the third of his missionary journeys, sometime during 54

A.D. We can assume that the apostle intended Galatians to be circulated among the Christian communities of that area.

1. The Challenge

As we saw earlier, the Pauline churches received Gentile converts into their midst without requiring them to be circumcised or to comply with Jewish dietary restrictions. However, it is circumcision that became the symbol of a challenge faced by Paul in guiding his Christian communities. After all, Jesus of Nazareth and all of his early followers, including Paul himself, were observant Jews. Many converts were Pharisees and some were apparently Essenes, all living in strict conformity with Jewish law. All of these, including Jesus himself (Lk 2:21), were circumcised. Furthermore, the "scriptures" of the Christian churches were the Hebrew Bible which enshrined the very requirements Paul was abandoning. We can see why many Christian communities maintained the observance of the Jewish law.

Now some of these conservative Christians had arrived in Galatia, most likely from the churches in Judea, insisting on the more rigorous requirements observed in their communities. These troublemakers were referred to as the "Judaizers" and Paul saw them as a challenge to his leadership and authority. To say that Paul was upset is to put it mildly. "I am astonished that you are so quickly deserting the one who called you . . . and are turning to a different gospel" (1:6). And even more pointedly, "You foolish Galatians! Who has bewitched you?" (3:1). The matter at hand is one that will continually plague the apostle throughout his missionary career. However, it is among the Galatians that the challenge seems to have been the most acute.

2. Paul's Response

First, the apostle felt called upon to present his credentials, to authenticate his standing as an authorized source for Christ's teaching. In doing this, he recounts his conversion and his mission (1:11–24), pointing out that "God, who had set me apart before I was born and called me through his grace, was pleased to reveal his Son to me, so that I might proclaim him among the Gentiles" (1:15–16).

Paul then gives his version of the crucial meeting on this very matter held in Jerusalem five years earlier (2:1–10), a meeting he felt approved his position and, most importantly, made no requirement of his Gentile converts to follow the Jewish code. "They asked only one thing, that we remember the poor, which was actually what I was eager to do" (2:10). If the matter had been settled in so clear-cut a manner, one wonders why the controversy continued.

However, Paul's account differs from the version found in Acts (15:1–29) where the decision required the Gentile converts "[to] abstain from what has been sacrificed to idols and from blood and from what is strangled and from fornication" (15:29). Indeed, it is Peter who proposes this compromise position. What Acts may be recounting is a moderate solution to the question worked out in subsequent years, a solution Paul was either unaware of or one with which he did not agree.

In any event, in spite of either decision, Paul later has a confrontation with Peter. "But when Cephas [Peter] came to Antioch, I opposed him to his face, because he stood self-condemned; for until certain people came from James, he used to eat with the Gentiles. But after they came, he drew back and kept himself separate for fear of the circumcision faction" (2:11–12). The matter was obviously not universally agreed to, and the arrival of the Judaizers in Galatia is further evidence of this.

Paul now lays down what is the core of his response to the challenge he faces: "a person is justified not by the works of the law but through faith [trust] in Jesus Christ" (2:16). He is careful to spell out just what this means in the present controversy. "Listen! I, Paul, am telling you that if you let yourselves be circumcised, Christ will be of no benefit to you. For in Christ Jesus neither circumcision nor uncircumcision counts for anything; the only thing that counts is faith working through love" (5:2–6). Nor does Paul conceal his antipathy toward those who are upsetting his communities with their demand of conformity to Jewish law. "I wish those who unsettle you would castrate themselves!" (5:12).

Paul was convinced that the core of the Judaic tradition could be made meaningful to the Gentiles. However, if this was to be done, the tradition had to be freed of those restrictions the Gentiles found offensive and Paul himself regarded as unessential—a view not shared by the Jewish communities or the more conservative Christians, especially the Judaizers.

3. Summary

The churches of Galatia were likely the easternmost of Paul's communities and thus the ones most exposed to the conservative influence which was strongest in the mideast and in Jerusalem especially. The greater threat brought the stronger reaction. Later, in Romans, we shall see Paul take a similar position on the role of faith versus law, but treat with more circumspection those who held to the stricter observance of the latter.

Given the subsequent spread of Christianity into the Gentile world and the events that were to occur after 70 A.D., it is easy for us to see the advantages of Paul's innovation and of his defense of a Christianity freed of the restrictions of the law. However, for those acutely aware of the roots of the new religion in Judaism and of the advantages in maintaining close ties with this inheritance, Paul's position was not all that obvious. Indeed, it could easily be seen as a dangerous threat.

It is obvious from the apostle's letter that Christian communities of Galatia found themselves caught up in a clash between these two views, between the guidance of their founder and the admonitions of revered leaders from the more tradition-bound churches. It could hardly have been easy for the Galatian Christians to know who was right. One can speculate on the divisive effect on these early churches of such a dispute.

C. PHILIPPI

SUGGESTED READING: ACTS 16:9–40; PHILIPPIANS

Paul visited Philippi during his second missionary journey just after he had crossed over into Europe for the first time. Philippi, in Macedonia, was a most famous city. Nearby, Mark Antony defeated Brutus and Cassius in a climactic battle and Antony himself was crushed there as well in the struggle that enabled his former ally, Octavian, to become Emperor Augustus Caesar. The city was a military colony of mixed population, including Jews. Paul established his first European community in Philippi in 50 A.D., and it would appear that some of the community's members were persons of influence, as we can see from his letter to the Philippians. (4:22). Paul subsequently praises the church for its continuing support of his mission (4:15–16).

As with the letter to the Galatians, Paul is on his third missionary journey and is writing to the Philippians from a prison cell in Ephesus (1:13), around 55 A.D. We do not know the reason for his incarceration but the Acts of the Apostles (19:23–40) gives a detailed description of a riot resulting from Paul's preaching, though saying nothing of an imprisonment. The letter has a rambling quality, which may mean it was written over a period of time or is a conflation of two or more letters.

1. The Letter

The opening of Philippians is unusual for an authentic Pauline letter: "Paul and Timothy, servants of Christ Jesus, to all the saints in Christ Jesus who are in Philippi, with the bishops and deacons"

(1:1). These titles, "bishops" and "deacons," are translations of the Greek words for "overseers" and "assistants" and most likely at this point had no specifically religious meaning. Their use by Paul, however, may indicate that the Christian community in Philippi was beginning to reflect a new form of church organization that would become more common as time passed. As it was the first community founded by Paul in a very Hellenized area, this development and the use of Greek secular titles is not surprising. The mideastern Christian communities, in contrast, continued to reflect the synagogue organization where the leaders were called "elders" or "presbyters" (Acts 11:30; 14:23; 15:2).

As was so frequently the case with these early Christian communities, the church in Philippi was running into opposition, and Paul wrote to encourage them in time of trial. But there was also an internal danger—growing divisions within the community itself. Paul urges, "Make my joy complete: be of the same mind, having the same love, being in full accord and of one mind" (2:2).

The source of the trouble is a familiar one, the continuing effort of the Judaizers to impose strict observance of the Jewish law on the Christian community. "Beware of the dogs, beware of the evil workers, beware of those who mutilate the flesh!" (3:2). Such mutilation must be circumcision, a harsh depiction of the revered Jewish practice coming from the apostle who, after all, was so marked himself.

Paul warmly compliments the Philippians on their generosity and support over the years (4:14–16) since he first visited them at the beginning of his missionary efforts in Europe. The letter shows the apostle's continuing concern for the Christians of Philippi.

2. The Nature of Christ

One passage in Philippians (2:6–11) reveals a surprising level of sophistication in the understanding of the gospel message.

Though he was in the form of God,
did not regard equality with God
as something to be exploited,

But emptied himself, taking the form of a slave,
being born in human likeness.

And being found in human form,
he humbled himself
and became obedient to the point of death—even death on a cross.

Therefore
God also highly exalted him
and gave him the name that is above every name,

So that at the name of Jesus
every knee should bend,
in heaven and on earth and under the earth,
and every tongue should confess that Jesus Christ is Lord,
to the glory of God the Father.

It is generally agreed that Paul is quoting a Christian hymn familiar to his readers, one perhaps used during community worship services. Recalling that "Lord" ("Kyrios" in the Greek) was substituted for the name of God in the Septuagint, the climactic avowal of the hymn is testimony to the Philippians' growing awareness of Christ's divinity.

Jews and Jewish Christians, as well, who had the absolute "one-ness of God" drilled into them, would not have tolerated any hint of a duality in the divine. Non-Jews, raised in a polytheistic environment and where gods frequently were said to have appeared in human form, would not have had as much difficulty accepting Jesus as a divine being. Reconciling a strict monotheism with the belief in Christ's divinity was a continuing challenge for the early church. Three centuries later, under the aegis of the first Christian emperor, the church's leaders will gather to face this very problem.

The community of Christians that inspired this most charming letter of Paul was obviously very much a part of the prevailing Hellenistic culture. It was testimony to the apostle's conviction that the message of Jesus, freed from the limitations of the Jewish culture, could reach the Gentile world. However, as we shall now see, Christians living in that world faced a formidable challenge.

STUDY QUESTIONS

1. How does Paul use the word "church" in his authentic letters?
2. What does Paul mean by the word "gospel" in his letters?
3. What is the "parousia" and what does Paul expect of it when he writes to the Thessalonians?
4. What challenge prompted Paul to write to the Galatian communities?
5. What was Paul's response to this challenge?
6. Wasn't this matter settled much earlier? Why has it cropped up again?
7. What is unusual about the opening used by Paul in writing to the Philippians? What might it indicate?
8. What is so striking about the passage 2:6–11 in Philippians?
9. When will the church deal definitively with this matter?

IV

The Pauline Communities
of the Apostolic Age: Corinth

A. THE CHURCH IN CORINTH

SUGGESTED READING: 1 CORINTHIANS 1:1–11:34

No church has left us a more complete picture of itself than the one revealed in Paul's letters to the Christians in Corinth. The city could rightly be described as the crossroads of the Roman empire. It lies on the isthmus between Macedonia and Achaia, a narrow barrier separating the Ionian and Aegean seas. Trans-shipping cargo at Corinth avoided a long sail around Achaia. The capital of this province, Corinth, was wealthy, cosmopolitan and noted for its art and architecture. (Even today, the city's ruins are impressive.) Also a sports center, the Corinthian games drew contestants from all over the empire.

Unfortunately, like port cities throughout history, Corinth had an unsavory reputation. To "go Corinthian" was a euphemism in the empire for licentious behavior. Calling a woman a "Corinthian" was to designate her a prostitute. The temple to Aphrodite Pandemus overlooked the city and was staffed by some one thousand prostitutes involved in the temple's orgiastic rituals, a circumstance which certainly contributed much to the city's shady image. In the face of such unlikely prospects, Paul established a thriving Christian church among the polyglot citizenry of the port city.

The apostle had arrived there in 51 A.D. on his second missionary journey, just after his disappointing reception in Athens.

As usual Paul first went to the Jewish community and enjoyed a modest success. Soon, however, his teachings turned that community against him and he shifted his efforts to the Gentiles. It was these converts who apparently formed the nucleus of Corinth's Christian community.

Some six years later, while on his third missionary journey, Paul was in Ephesus when he heard of the problems developing in the Corinthian church. 1 Corinthians was the apostle's response to what he had heard and it is virtually a catalogue of admonitions concerning their conduct. In the letter Paul gives us our clearest picture of a Pauline community in the mid-first century of our era. Keeping in touch with events in Corinth through intermediaries, Paul wrote again about a year later, this time from Philippi. 2 Corinthians, however, may be a compilation of more than one letter.

1. Factionalism

As we see from 1 Corinthians the local church was being divided by conflicting loyalties. "What I mean is that each of you says, 'I belong to Paul,' or 'I belong to Apollos,' or 'I belong to Cephas,' or 'I belong to Christ' " (1:12). As the church there could well have been made up of more than one group, these factions might have involved Christians who worshiped together, small communities making up the larger one.

Apollos is mentioned in Acts (18:24) as "an eloquent man." He was an impressive figure—a converted Jew from Alexandria, a city renowned as a center of Jewish scholarship. Apollos seems to have come to an incomplete understanding of Jesus' message and was then further enlightened by Paul's associates, Priscilla and Aquila. He eventually ended up in Corinth where he apparently picked up a following. The reference to "Cephas" (Peter) would indicate the presence of more conservative Christians, Jewish or Gentiles who had first been converts to Judaism.

Those who "belong to Christ" are difficult to pinpoint; they might have been Christians who felt they had some special relationship to Christ, making them independent of local church leadership. If such were the case, then we might have an early appearance of the "Gnostics," an heretical Christian sect that will be so troublesome to the churches later in the century. We sometimes have the impression that the early Christian communities were one, big, happy family. That is not the picture Paul leaves us with in 1 and 2 Corinthians.

Paul's continued stress on church unity is a reflection of this factionalism. He meets it by stressing his own authority. "What would you prefer? Am I to come to you with a stick, or with love in a spirit of gentleness?" (4:21). You get the impression that Paul could have played it both ways. Given the strains on the unity of the Corinthian church, it was likely that only the apostle's personal authority held it together.

2. The Pagan Influence

The Corinthian Christians could hardly isolate themselves from their pagan environment—something that Paul himself was fully aware of. "I wrote to you in my letter (one written prior to 1 Corinthians but no longer extant) not to associate with sexually immoral persons—not at all meaning the immoral of this world, or the greedy and robbers, or idolaters, since you would then need to go out of the world" (5:9–10).

Many, if not most, of these Christians were converts, and they could not easily shed the habits of their earlier lives. It is hard for us, living in a world strongly influenced by Christianity, to appreciate the challenges facing these newly baptized members of the church. The problems taken up by Paul in 1 and 2 Corinthians have their source in the conflict between the pagan milieu and gospel message.

a. An Illicit Marriage

Paul cites the case of a Christian living with his father's wife (not necessarily his own mother à la Oedipus), a situation that could have existed before his conversion, but is forbidden now. The Corinthian Christians were apparently tolerant of the situation, but Paul was not. He had already "pronounced judgment in the name of the Lord Jesus on the man who has done such a thing . . . you are to hand this man over to Satan for the destruction of the flesh, so that his spirit may be saved in the day of the Lord" (5:3-5). It should be noted that Paul effects this "excommunication" on his own authority, again the direct and personal authority he exercised over the communities he had founded.

b. Suing in a Civil Court

Some Corinthian Christians continued to make use of the civil courts when in conflict with a fellow Christian. Proneness to sue is not a modern phenomenon. Paul sees in this practice a failure to recognize the true nature of church. "I say this to your shame. Can it be that there is no one among you wise enough to decide between one believer and another, but a believer goes to court against a believer—and before unbelievers at that?" (6:5-6). The unity between Christians was contradicted by such suits, and Paul forbids them.

c. Law and License

In those Christian communities where the Jewish culture still exerted a strong influence, such as the churches in Galatia, Paul could say, "a person is justified not by the works of the law but through faith in Jesus Christ" (Gal 2:16). But in 1 Corinthians such a remark could be interpreted as freedom from all restraints, and Paul is careful to correct such an impression. " 'All things are lawful for me,' but not all things are beneficial. 'All things are lawful for me,' but I will not be dominated by anything. . . . Shun fornication!" (6:12, 18).

In the licentious atmosphere of Corinth, against which a modern port city would pale, it could not have been easy for some new Christians to follow the apostle's admonition. To us the apostle's advice might seem extreme. "But because of cases of sexual immorality, each man should have his own wife and each woman her own husband. To the unmarried and the widows I say that it is well for them to remain unmarried as I am. But if they are not practicing self-control, they should marry. For it is better to marry than to be aflame with passion" (7:2, 8–9). However, we have to keep in mind that the Corinthian Christians were being called upon to live in a manner quite at variance with the society around them.

It is no doubt this same atmosphere that led Paul to urge a stable lifestyle. "However that may be, let each of you lead the life that the Lord has assigned, to which God called you. This is my rule in all the churches" (7:17). Perhaps startling to us was his application of this advice even to the slaves. "Were you a slave when called? Do not be concerned about it. Even if you can gain your freedom, make use of your present condition now more than ever" (7:21).

d. Divorce and the Mixed Marriage

But what of the difficult situation where a Christian is married to a non-Christian. In contrast to the Jewish and Gentile cultures which allowed the married to divorce, the Christian communities did not. In 1 Corinthians (7:12–13) Paul agrees that as long as the unbelieving partner is willing to live at peace with the believer, there is not to be a divorce. However, if such is not the case, then separation is permitted. "But if the unbelieving partner separates, let it be so; in such a case the brother or sister is not bound" (7:15). It is not difficult to imagine the turmoil, even tragedy, that could follow when a Jew or Gentile became a Christian.

e. Meat and Scandal

At the time, much of the fresh meat available in the city's markets came from animals used in pagan rituals. Could Christians buy and eat such items? Paul must deal with the problem: "Now concerning food sacrificed to idols . . ." (8:1). Some Christians, he knows, fully aware that "no idol in the world really exists, and that there is no God but one" (8:4), did not hesitate to each such meat. However, others "have become so accustomed to idols until now, they still think of the food they eat as food offered to an idol; and their conscience, being weak, is defiled" (8:7). Paul calls on the more knowledgeable Christian to "take care that this liberty of yours does not somehow become a stumbling block to the weak" (8:9). Yet Paul does not make avoiding such meat a hard and fast rule: "Eat whatever is sold in the meat market without raising any question on the ground of conscience" (10:25). However, the overriding principle must be, "Do not seek your own advantage, but that of the other" (10:24). Should eating such meat cause scandal, "do not eat it . . . for the sake of conscience—I mean the other's conscience, not your own" (10:28–29). Paul does not hesitate to reflect this in his own conduct. "I will never eat meat, so that I may not cause one of them to fall" (8:13).

f. The Role of Women in Worship

In Jewish worship, in both the temple and the synagogue, women had a largely passive role, much as it is in the more conservative Jewish groups today. However, in the pagan sects, the parts played by women were not so limited. Indeed, in certain instances, they were central to religious services. It appears that this more active participation of women carried over into Christian worship. In 1 Corinthians the focus of this seems to be whether or not the woman's head is covered and Paul makes his position clear: "any woman who prays or prophesies with her head unveiled disgraces her head" (11:5).

It is interesting and revealing that Paul defends his position by pointing out: "But if anyone is disposed to be contentious—we have no such custom, nor do the churches of God" (11:16). Could it be that Paul was concerned about the liberalism of the Corinthian community scandalizing other Christian communities? This might account for his even stronger admonition later on. "As in all the churches of the saints, women should be silent in the churches. For they are not permitted to speak. . . . For it is shameful for a woman to speak in church" (14:33–35). Given today's heated discussion of the role of women in the liturgy, we can easily imagine the reception that Paul's admonition received in Corinth.

3. Eucharist

We are indebted to 1 Corinthians for the earliest scriptural references to the eucharist. Paul is concerned that some of the Christian community are still participating in "the worship of idols" (10:14), a practice he regards as violating the fundamental unity of the church as symbolized by the eucharist. "The cup of blessing that we bless, is it not a sharing in the blood of Christ? The bread that we break, is it not a sharing in the body of Christ? Because there is one bread, we who are many are one body, for we all partake of the one bread" (10:16–17).

There is evidence that, from the very earliest days, Christians gathered for "the breaking of the bread" (Acts 2:42,46; 20:7). It would appear that this rite was the focus of the Corinthian church's assemblies, as it must have been for the gatherings of the other Christian communities. Paul gives us the formula which was used in his churches. Interestingly, each record we have of the eucharistic prayer varies from the others (Mk 14:22–25; Mt 26:26–30; Lk 22:19–20).

Paul, reflecting the ritual used in his churches, gives the eucharistic formula as follows: "For I received from the Lord what I also handed on to you, that the Lord Jesus on the night when he was betrayed took a loaf of bread, and when he had given thanks, he broke it and said, 'This is my body that is for you. Do this in remembrance of me.' In the same way he took the cup also, after supper, saying, 'This cup is the new covenant in my blood. Do this, as often as you drink it, in remembrance of me' " (11:23–25).

However, what was meant to be a sign of Christian unity had become something quite different in Corinth. "For, to begin with, when you come together as a church, I hear that there are divisions among you; and to some extent I believe it. Indeed, there have to be factions among you, for only so will it become clear who among you are genuine" (11:18–19). However inevitable such factions might be, some conduct is reprehensible for the Christian. Paul particularly singles out the neglect of the poor by the rich. "When you come together, it is not really to eat the Lord's supper. For when the time comes to eat, each of you goes ahead with your own supper, and one goes hungry and another becomes drunk. . . . Or do you show contempt for the church of God and humiliate those who have nothing?" (11:20–22).

The eucharistic liturgy had its roots in the paschal meal of the Jews. However, these ritual meals, an early form of the "pot-luck" supper, were also common in pagan ceremonies. But some of these rituals were excessive, even orgiastic, a tendency that Gentile converts could have carried over into early forms of Christian worship. In the next century Christians would find themselves accused of bizarre practices during their gatherings. This fact and the abuses Paul pointed out led to the communal meal held in connection with the eucharist being abandoned.

STUDY QUESTIONS

1. What were the chief features of the city of Corinth?
2. What were some of the factions dividing the Christian community in Corinth?
3. What problems were created in Corinth by the influence of a pagan environment?
4. Was there a special problem created by women in the worship services of the Corinthian Christians?
5. What did Paul object to about the eucharists held in Corinth?

V

The Pauline Communities
of the Apostolic Age:
Corinth (Cont.), Philemon and Romans

A. CORINTH (Cont.)

1. The Gifts of the Spirit

SUGGESTED READING: I CORINTHIANS 12:1–14:40

a. The Gifts and Unity

So far we have seen how Paul had to struggle to preserve the unity of the Corinthian church, threatened as it was by factionalism, the persistence of pagan influences, disparities of wealth, even the role of women in liturgy. Now the apostle must confront a further challenge stemming from the very spiritual gifts that blessed the community and its ministries: "the utterance of wisdom . . . the utterance of knowledge . . . faith . . . healing . . . the working of miracles . . . prophecy . . . the discernment of spirits . . . the interpretation of tongues" (12:8–10). The ministries or offices in the community Paul mentions are "apostles . . . prophets . . . teachers . . . deeds of power . . . healing . . . assistance . . . leadership . . . various kinds of tongues" (12:28). What is important, however, as Paul stresses, is that each gift or ministry "is given . . . for the common good" (12:7).

We have no clear idea as to the nature of some of the special gifts or offices, but it is hardly difficult for us to see how they could lead to disunity with each person pursuing his or her own goal and

126

interests, perhaps even jealous of the gifts and responsibilities accorded to others. In response to this threat, Paul uses the analogy between the church and the human body. "For just as the body is one and has many members, and all the members of the body, though many, are one body, so it is with Christ. For in the one Spirit we were all baptized into one body—Jews or Greeks, slaves or free—and we were all made to drink of one Spirit" (12:12–13).

The deepest divisions in the community were between the Jews and the Gentiles and between those who were free men and women and those who were slaves. If the church could achieve a unity among these groups, then, certainly, the other divisions could be bridged as well. It is in this context that Paul gives us his most beautiful passage on the fundamental element in Christian unity:

"If I speak in the tongues of mortals and of angels, but do not have love, I am a noisy gong or a clanging cymbal. And if I have prophetic powers, and understand all mysteries and all knowledge, and if I have all faith, so as to remove mountains, but do not have love, I am nothing. If I give away all my possessions, and if I hand over my body so that I may boast, but do not have love, I gain nothing.

"Love is patient; love is kind; love is not envious or boastful or arrogant or rude. It does not insist on its own way; it is not irritable or resentful; it does not rejoice in wrongdoing, but rejoices in the truth. It bears all things, believes all things, hopes all things, endures all things. Love never ends. . . . And now faith, hope, and love abide, these three; and the greatest of these is love" (13:1–8, 13).

b. The Problem of "Tongues"

Unintelligible utterances during religious exaltation were found in both Hellenistic and eastern religions at the time of Paul and, given the background of some of the Corinthian Christians, it is not surprising that the practice would have found its way into their worship services. The apostle, as we see in 1 Corinthians, at no time rejects this practice: "For those who speak in a tongue do not speak to other people but to God; for nobody understands them, since they are speaking mysteries in the Spirit" (14:2). A number of

Christian traditions maintained such a practice into the present time. In fact, there has been a recent resurgence of "speaking in tongues" among groups usually referred to as "charismatics."

However, Paul recognizes the necessity of some control lest it get out of hand. An excess of "tongues" could have an unfortunate effect. "If, therefore, the whole church comes together and all speak in tongues, and outsiders or unbelievers enter, will they not say that you are out of your mind?" (14:23). For this reason, the apostle suggests a careful "programming" of the Christian worship service. "What should be done then, my friends? When you come together, each one has a hymn, a lesson, a revelation, a tongue, or an interpretation. Let all things be done for building up. . . . But if there is no one to interpret, let them be silent in church and speak to themselves and to God" (14:26–28).

In reviewing Paul's admonitions and guidelines for the Corinthian church, one can gather that participation in that community's worship must have been a heady experience. When we reflect on the array of different ethnic populations, cultures, religions and social strata that made up the cities of the empire, we can appreciate the challenge faced by the apostle in his efforts to create Christian communities in these metropolitan areas. Even to convey something central to the gospel would face formidable obstacles.

2. Resurrection

SUGGESTED READING: I CORINTHIANS 15:1–58

a. The Challenge

When Paul spoke to the Athenians in Agora, we are told (Acts 17:22ff) that he held his audience's attention until he mentioned the resurrection of Jesus. Hearing this, his audience departed, some sneering, others with a more polite rejection. The lengthy treatment Paul gives the resurrection in 1 Corinthians (15:1–58) demonstrates his conviction that a similar skepticism existed in Corinth as well.

The matter in question is absolutely essential. "If Christ has not been raised, your faith is futile and you are still in your sins. Then those also who have died in Christ have perished. If for this life only we have hoped in Christ, we are of all people most to be pitied" (15:17–19). Yet, there were some in the community who harbored doubts. "Now if Christ is proclaimed as raised from the dead, how can some of you say there is no resurrection of the dead?" (15:12). This rejection of a central Christian doctrine springs from a fundamental difference between the Hellenistic and semitic cultures.

b. *The Jewish View*

For the Semites in general and the Jews in particular, all living things, including humanity, are animated matter. This is evidenced in the description of the creation of Adam found in Genesis. "The Lord God formed man from the dust of the ground, and breathed into his nostrils the breath of life; and the man became a living being" (2:7). At death, this breath or spirit of God is withdrawn and the body returns to its original state. "You are dust, and to dust you shall return" (Gen 3:19).

For the Jews, in the early years, the only notion of survival that could be envisioned was through one's family, tribe or people. In time, however, another possibility arose, a reconstitution of the body and a return to it of God's spirit, the breath of life. A vivid description of "resurrection" is found in the prophet Ezekiel's "Vision of the Dry Bones" (1:1–12). Some Jewish contemporaries of Jesus and Paul were looking forward to a personal restoration, a reanimation of the body, or resurrection. But the matter was hotly debated between the Sadducees and Pharisees. Paul, himself a Pharisee, was in agreement with them as we have seen.

c. *The Hellenistic View*

In contrast, the Hellenic culture, particularly under the influence of the philosopher Plato, saw humanity as a combination of matter and spirit, the material and immaterial elements. However, matter was a limitation placed on the spiritual element and death was seen as a liberation of the spirit from such limitations. It is possible that such a view had its origins in the Far East where the material is often denigrated in deference to the spiritual.

For the Hellenists, then, a bodily resurrection represented a return of the spirit to its former imprisonment in the material. Such a prospect would hardly make much sense, and even less would it be something to be hoped for. From Paul's letter it is obvious that some of the Corinthians, influenced by their Greek heritage, have come to this conclusion.

d. Paul's Solution: The Spiritual Body

For Paul, Jesus' resurrection is a fact, witnessed personally. "Last of all, as to one untimely born, he appeared also to me" (15:8). And, through the raising of Jesus, the Christian is to be raised. "For as all die in Adam, so all will be made alive in Christ" (15:22). But there still remains the question, "How are the dead raised? With what kind of body do they come?" (15:35). Paul recognizes the difficulty some of his readers would have with a simple restoration of the condition prior to death, a "reanimation."

His solution is innovative. "So it is with the resurrection of the dead. What is sown is perishable, what is raised is imperishable. . . . It is sown a physical body, it is raised a spiritual body. If there is a physical body, there is also a spiritual body" (15:42–44). Such a body, in Paul's view, would not be a limitation on the spirit. Incorruptible, free from decay, the spiritual body would be a fulfillment. "Death has been swallowed up in victory. Where, O death, is your victory? Where, O death, is your sting? But thanks be to God, who gives us the victory through our Lord Jesus Christ" (15:54–57).

3. The Parousia

We have already seen evidence of the early Christians' concern about the parousia in our discussion of 1 Thessalonians. Here Paul again shares with his community the conviction that the final day will soon arrive. "Listen, I will tell you a mystery! We will not all die, but we will all be changed, in a moment, in the twinkling of an eye, at the last trumpet" (15:51–52). An expectation of the return of Christ must have affected the lives of the Corinthian Christians, but it seems for Paul in 1 Corinthians that there is less urgency. He closes with words obviously meant to calm: "Therefore, my beloved, be steadfast, immovable, always excelling in the work of the Lord, because you know that in the Lord your labor is not in vain" (15:58).

4. 2 Corinthians

SUGGESTED READING: 2 CORINTHIANS

On receiving a report on conditions in Corinth from his companion, Titus, Paul wrote to the community from Macedonia. The letter reveals far more about Paul himself than it does of the recipients. It is the most subjective of his writings. However, the letter does reflect a change in the Corinthian church. "For even if I made you sorry with my letter, I do not regret it.... Now I rejoice, not because you were grieved, but because your grief led to repentance" (7:8–9).

All is not completely well. Others have come "proclaiming another Jesus than the one we proclaimed" (11:4), and the Corinthians "submit to it readily enough" (11:4). These "super-apostles," as Paul calls them, are influencing their hearers, and the apostle now intends to come to Corinth personally to survey the damage. To prepare for what was his third and final visit, Paul admonishes his followers: "Examine yourselves to see whether you are living in the faith. Test yourselves" (13:5).

5. Summary

The Christian community in Corinth was in many ways unique. The raucous and riotous character of the port city would assure that. However, the church must have shared characteristics found in the other Pauline communities where gospel came into contact with the Hellenistic culture. Intermixed with the prevalent paganism, these early Christians must have had many of the same problems and faced the same challenges.

Factionalism surely plagued every such community whose members were drawn from the various ethnic groups—a challenge made the more acute if Jews were included, as they usually were. Then there were the other Christian missionaries who challenged Paul and his version of the gospel, the Judaizers being the most troublesome. More radical influences, such as the Gnostics, only aggravated the problem.

Many members of these early churches were only a few years, or even less, from living as Gentiles in a pagan world. In the same place, still among their family and friends, they struggled to live the Christian faith—not an easy task where even deciding whether or not to eat meat could challenge one's convictions. Nor could they easily strip themselves of former customs as they entered a new community. Women would seem to have presented a special problem in this regard when it came to worship services. The difficulties created by "tongues" may have been something carried over from earlier involvement in ecstatic religious practices.

All these communities certainly felt the controlling hand of Paul striving by his personal influence and authority to stave off disintegration. Yet other forces were at work. There was the gospel itself. In spite of disputes, the core of Jesus' message must have been shared by all. The eucharist, again despite difficulties, brought the church together for weekly worship. Ministries within the communities and spiritual gifts, though sometimes a challenge to unity, must have begun to develop into the local authority that was soon to replace the unifying influence of Paul.

B. PHILEMON

SUGGESTED READING: PHILEMON

In 61 A.D. Paul arrived in Rome as a prisoner and remained under house arrest for two years. From this time we have a final example of the personal touch by which Paul must have guided not only his communities but even individual members. His letter to Philemon, a wealthy and influential Christian layman living in Colossae, may well be characteristic of other such correspondence no longer extant. Onesimus, a slave of Philemon's, escaped and eventually became a convert of Paul's and was of service to him. Paul urges Philemon to take Onesimus back without punishment.

Besides showing us a tender side of the apostle, the letter reminds us of the problems that must have arisen in Pauline communities where slaves and freemen were regarded equally as members. As we saw earlier, it was no simple task to make a reality of Paul's own dictum in Galatians, "There is no longer slave or free . . . for all of you are one in Christ Jesus" (3:28). One wonders if any other groups of the period attempted to meet such a challenge.

C. ROMANS

There remains one letter which scholars agree was written by Paul. However, unlike the letters we have already seen, Romans was addressed to a community the apostle had not founded and not as yet visited. As Paul was intending to come to the capital of the empire in the near future, he wrote to the Roman Christian community in order to introduce himself while in Corinth during the winter of 57–58 A.D.

Indirectly, Paul certainly knew a great deal about the Roman church, and his letter tells us much about the early period of a Christian community that will rise to such importance in the succeeding centuries. Because of its significance we will devote a chapter to the Roman community later in the book and discuss Romans at that time.

STUDY QUESTIONS

1. What did Paul regard as the greatest of the spiritual gifts?
2. What is the gift of "tongues" and what were some of its effects

on the Christian worship services? What were Paul's proposals regarding the exercise of this gift?

3. Why did the Jewish and Hellenistic cultures differ on the Christian belief in bodily resurrection?

4. How did Paul deal with this problem?

5. In writing to the church in Corinth does Paul still expect the proximate coming of the parousia?

6. Are there changes in the Corinthian community reflected in 2 Corinthians?

7. What does Paul's letter to Philemon concern?

VI

The Pauline Communities
of the Sub-Apostolic Age:
The Pastorals, Colossians and Ephesians

A. THE TRANSITION

We now come to the period that Father Raymond Brown (*The Churches the Apostles Left Behind,* p. 15) has designated as the "sub-apostolic period" or the final third of the first century, and with it a crucial transition has taken place. The "witnesses" have now passed from the scene. These were the first generation of Christians, which included those who had received the "good news" from Jesus himself (a claim that Paul had made in his own case; cf. Galatians 1:12). Paul's churches and their counterparts founded by other "witnesses" were now spread throughout the empire, some existing in radically different circumstances from others. It is most likely that, as the period opens, the "founding fathers" of these communities were dead, including Paul.

The "good news," as preached by the "witnesses" and the founders, had been subjected to varied interpretations, as we have seen from Paul's authentic letters. Like the apostle, we can assume that, during their lifetimes, the "witnesses" and founders, by their personal authority, we able to protect their churches from mistaken interpretations of the gospel. Now, however, in the sub-apostolic age, with their passing, the question arises: Who will be able to protect the gospel from distortion and misinterpretation?

135

B. THE PASTORALS

SUGGESTED READING: 1 AND 2 TIMOTHY, TITUS

1. Authorship

In the "Pastoral Letters," so titled because of their content, we see a response to the above challenge. Though 1 and 2 Timothy and Titus are attributed to Paul, the majority of scripture scholars today question their Pauline authorship. The language, style and theological content of these letters indicate an author sufficiently familiar with Paul's life and teachings to be able to clothe himself in the apostle's mantle of authority. The author, however, writes under circumstances different from those of the apostle, reflecting a period later than that of Paul, perhaps in the 80s. In the Hebrew Bible, we saw how with the book of Isaiah, the writings of subsequent authors were attributed to their prestigious predecessor. As these subsequent works brought the thoughts of the original prophet to bear on later conditions, carrying on his work, as it were, nothing was regarded as wrong about such an attribution. We shall find other examples of this practice as the New Testament is formed.

In Acts, a person called Timothy is described as a constant companion of Paul. He was a convert to Christianity "the son of a Jewish woman who was a believer; but his father was a Greek" (16:1). He is also referred to in Paul's letters. Titus too, identified in Galatians (2:3) as a Gentile, is seen from the apostle's letters to be Paul's trusted companion. 1 Timothy (1:3) shows Timothy as occupying a position of authority in Ephesus. Titus, in the letter addressed to him, has a similar role in Crete. The actual author of the Pastorals, aware of these traditions about Timothy and Titus, could have addressed the correspondence to them in order to give verisimilitude to the letters.

2. The Challenge

The problem facing these sub-apostolic age churches is made clear in the Pastorals. In 1 Timothy, the recipient of the letter is to "instruct certain people not to teach any different doctrine, and not to occupy themselves with myths . . . that promote speculations" (1:3–4). Similarly in Titus we are told, "There are also many rebellious people, idle talkers and deceivers" (1:10), and in 2 Timothy, "Hold to the standard of sound teaching that you have heard from me" (1:13). Obviously, deviant versions of the "good news" are being circulated within these Pauline communities, preached by self-styled teachers. What can be done to protect the membership of the church from false doctrines?

Of course such a challenge is not peculiar to religious groups in general. In any institution, founded by a charismatic figure, a crisis usually arises when that person leaves the scene. How can the integrity of the founding vision be preserved, especially when the organization or community is faced with new conditions and challenges unforeseen by the founder himself? The response is almost universal; the vision is encapsulated in a tradition or even a written document, and its preservation is entrusted to an authority responsible for the correct interpretation of the tradition. The manner of selecting and structuring this authority will vary but the purpose is the same; to see that in adaptations to new circumstances and challenges, the essentials of the original vision are preserved. We see an example of this in our own history. Preserving the vision of the founding fathers is entrusted to the executive, legislative and judicial branches of the government.

3. The Response

In the light of what has just been said, the Pastorals should not be seen so much as letters written to individuals but rather as addressed to communities in order to reinforce the authority of their leadership. The author of the Pastorals has cloaked himself with the authority of Paul and has addressed two men known to have been the apostle's disciples and who could have exercised leadership roles after the death of Paul.

In the Pastorals, Timothy and Titus are depicted as leaders in their respective communities and entrusted with the responsibility of preserving the true traditions: "Timothy, guard what has been entrusted to you. Avoid the profane chatter and contradictions of what is falsely called knowledge" (1 Tim 6:20). "Now you have observed my teaching" (2 Tim 3:10). "He must have a firm grasp of the word that is trustworthy in accordance with the teaching, so that he may be able both to preach with sound doctrine" (Tit 1:9). The reference in 1 Timothy to "what is falsely called knowledge" may be the early appearance of what became the most serious challenge of the early Christian Church in the latter part of the first and all of the second century.

The "Gnostics" (from the Greek word for knowledge, "gnosis") were Christians who claimed to have special revelation from God, or Christ, or even Paul, which challenged the traditions of the "main line" Christian communities. In 1945 a Gnostic library was discovered near Naj Hammadi in Egypt, giving us a clearer picture of this movement which is sometimes called the "First Heresy." In the light of their special "knowledge" the Gnostics proposed various, often bizarre, interpretations of Christ's message. In combating the threat the author or authors of the Pastorals evoke the authority of the church's leadership. The Pastorals also give us a clearer picture of the form that leadership was to take.

4. Elders and Bishops

Earlier we saw in Philippians a mention of the "bishop" as a church leader, translating the Greek, "episcopoi" or "overseer." Whether such a title was formal or simply descriptive at that time we do not know. However, in the Pastorals there is no question but that "bishop" is the formal title of a church leader. In 1 Timothy (3:1–7) the qualifications of one holding such position are given at length. The picture is more complex in Titus where the community leader is referred to as both "presbyter," from the Greek for "elder," and as "bishop." A further complication is found in 1 Timothy (4:14) where a group of "presbyters" select the "bishop."[3]

Two influences may be at work here. The Gentile Christians would have tended to choose the neutral Greek, "overseer" (bishop), though it should be noted that in the "Dead Sea Scrolls" leaders of the Essene communities were called "overseers." If, as is suspected, members of this group became Christians, they also could have been the source of the title "bishop" being given to leaders of the church. Jewish Christians, on the other hand, familiar with the synagogue organization, would have used the title given to the leaders in that community, i.e. "elder" or "presbyter." It would appear that for a time these titles were interchangeable, and only later did "presbyter" become the designation of a specific group among the leadership.[3]

5. Responsibilities of Leadership

The Pastorals are clear on the most important responsibility of the "bishop/presbyter": it is to "hold fast to the mystery of the faith with a clear conscience" (1 Tim 3:9) and "to encourage men to follow sound doctrine and to refute those who contradict it" (Tit 1:9). The author of Titus speaks plainly. He identifies the trouble-makers as being "especially those of the circumcision" (1:10). The controversies of Paul's time apparently continued. "They must be silenced, since they are upsetting whole families by teaching for sordid gain what it is not right to teach" (1:11). Further, "After a first and second admonition, have nothing more to do with anyone who causes divisions" (3:10). The person in question here is no doubt the supporter of a particular philosophical school whose argumentative attitude is upsetting the community, rather than a heretic in the modern sense.

The Pastorals are replete with admonitions as to how Christians are to conduct themselves in order "that we may lead a quiet and peaceable life in all godliness and dignity . . . without anger or argument" (1 Tim 2:2, 8). One's public conduct as a Christian must be similarly inoffensive. "Remind them to be subject to rulers and authorities, to be obedient, to be ready for every good work" (Tit 3:1). Strange advice coming from a successor of Paul who boasted of his run-ins with the law and was so often the source of civil disturbance—further evidence that with the Pastorals we find the Christian community in circumstances quite different from those of the apostolic age.

C. COLOSSIANS

SUGGESTED READING: THE LETTER TO THE COLOSSIANS

1. Authorship

The references in Colossians to Epaphras (1:7), Onesimus (4:7) and Aristarchus (4:10) show the author's familiarity with the letter to Philemon who was a Colossian. However, as we saw earlier, the majority of scripture scholars today do not regard Colossians as authentically Pauline. Again, in this view, we have a late first century author assuming the mantle of the apostle to meet the crisis that has arisen after the demise of Paul. The use of names found in the genuine Pauline letters would lend authenticity to the letter. However, if it did come from the hand of Paul, it would have been late in his life and perhaps when he himself was aware of the impending crisis that would follow his death. Also Colossians may well have been addressed to a broader audience than just one local church.

2. The Challenges

As we saw in the Pastorals, the threat being dealt with in Colossians is to the tradition, particularly its corruption by deviant teachings. "See to it that no one takes you captive through philosophy and empty deceit, according to human tradition, according to the elemental spirits of the universe, and not according to Christ" (2:8). Here the reference to the Gnostics is all the clearer.

We also find traces of other earlier conflicts. "Therefore do not let anyone condemn you in matters of food and drink or of observing festivals, new moons, or sabbaths" (2:16). Still present in the church are those who would reimpose some of the requirements of Jewish law onto the Christian community. But it is now made clear that faith in Jesus has replaced even the most fundamental requirement of the law. "In him [Jesus] also you were circumcised with a spiritual circumcision, by putting off the body of the flesh in the circumcision of Christ" (2:11).

3. The Parousia

We saw in the Pauline churches of the apostolic age an expectation of the parousia, a concern for the resurrection soon to occur. This expectation had now faded and had been replaced by the notion that there was a sense in which it had already taken place. The author of Colossians tells his readers to be grateful "to the Father, who has enabled you to share in the inheritance of the saints in the light. He has rescued us from the power of darkness and transferred us into the kingdom of his beloved Son, in whom we have redemption, the forgiveness of sins" (1:12–14).

The Christian has already attained in part to something originally thought to be entirely in the future. "So if you have been raised with Christ, seek the things that are above" (3:1). Further, "when you were buried with [Christ] in baptism, you were also raised with him" (2:12). If the Christian has already been "raised," then the "end" has already begun. What we have here is known as "realized eschatology."

The "eschaton" is the term used to refer to the final stage of human history. A "realized eschaton" refers to the belief that the parousia has already happened and the Christian is now in an interim state which will be fully realized later on. As the author of Colossians says, "Your life is hidden with Christ in God. When you were buried with him in baptism, you were also raised with him" (3:3–4). Later, at the turn of the century the gospel of John will give a more precise expression to this belief. "I am the resurrection and the life . . . everyone who lives and believes in me will never die" (11:25–26).

If Christians are now living in the "last of times," then their lives should reflect it. Orderly lives are required of Christian households, giving the impression that the author hopes to counteract an impression that something else was the case. "Wives, be subject to your husbands. . . . Husbands, love your wives. . . . Children, obey your parents. . . . Fathers, do not provoke your children. . . . Slaves, obey your earthly masters in everything. . . . Masters, treat your slaves justly and fairly" (3:18–22; 4:1). Such a focus on domestic tranquility may well indicate another change in the Christian community.

4. The Nature of Christ

As the century ends, Colossians reflects a clearer understanding of the nature of Christ. "He is the image of the invisible God . . . in him all things in heaven and on earth were created. . . . For in him the whole fullness of deity dwells bodily" (1:15–16; 2:9). Again we find ourselves getting closer to the language of the gospel of John. "In the beginning was the Word . . . and the Word was God. . . . All things came into being through him" (1:1–3). But if Christians are gaining a more profound grasp of Christ, it should not be surprising that Colossians reveals that they are also gaining a deeper understanding of their community.

5. The New Meaning of Church

In his authentic letters, Paul used the word "church" to refer exclusively to the local Christian community. For the apostle, there are simply "churches," one equal to the other. In Colossians, however, there is an entity referred to as "the church" which transcends the local community. "He [Christ] is the head of the body, the church" (1:18). In 1 Corinthians (12:12ff) Paul used the analogy of the body to deal with the interrelationships between various ministries within the local church. Now the analogy is to a wider reality. "There is no longer Greek and Jew, circumcised and uncircumcised, barbarian, Scythian, slave and free; but Christ is all and in all! And let the peace of Christ rule in your hearts, to which indeed you were called in the one body" (3:11-15).

The reference is not to a local community but to a reality that reaches out to all Christians. Indeed, a new group is embraced. "Scythian" is much like our word "barbarian," a hint that the church now extends beyond its previous limits, reaching out to those beyond the Greco-Roman culture. A new depth of unity embraces all the followers of Christ. We find it expressed in the author's poignant words, "In my flesh I am completing what is lacking in Christ's afflictions for the sake of his body, that is, the church" (1:24).

6. Leadership

In contrast to the Pastorals, Colossians makes no mention of an authoritative leadership. If the letter was meant for a wider readership than a single community or local church, perhaps even for the whole church, then the reason for the lack of such a leadership is understandable. There simply was no leader or leaders at that time whose authority would have been recognized by all of the local churches.

To maintain unity, to protect the church from false doctrine, the author could only appeal to that unity all Christians had in Christ. The inner reality of the church was the only assurance for the future. "The substance belongs to Christ . . . the whole body, nourished and held together by its ligaments and sinews, grows with a growth that is from God" (2:17–19). An inner unity must be the ultimate guarantor of the survival, in fact, of the traditions.

D. EPHESIANS

SUGGESTED READING: THE LETTER TO THE EPHESIANS

1. Authorship

As the century ends, another author writes in the name of Paul. Though Ephesians was written later than Colossians, the close parallels between the two letters would lead us to believe that Ephesians was addressed to the same audience. In fact, the earliest manuscripts of the letter we have do not indicate a destination, and other early sources list the letter as addressed to the Laodiceans. It is also the most impersonal of the letters in the Pauline canon, reinforcing the idea that Ephesians was not written by the apostle, but by an unknown hand for a general audience.

2. The Cosmic Christ

The letter reveals a community or group of communities that progressed beyond what we saw in Colossians. For them, Christ now has an even more exalted and cosmic role in salvation. "Blessed be the God and Father of our Lord Jesus Christ, who has blessed us in Christ with every spiritual blessing in the heavenly places . . . in him we have redemption through his blood, the forgiveness of our trespasses" (1:3–7). Christ's cosmic role is emphasized when the author speaks of a plan "to be carried out in the fullness of time: namely, to bring all things in the heavens and on earth into one under Christ's headship" (1:10).

3. The Church

As in Colossians, the church is no longer the local community but a transcendent and unifying reality. "[The Father] has put all things under his feet and has made him the head over all things for the church, which is his body, the fullness of him who fills all in all" (1:22–23). This universal human unity is achieved by Jesus' death. "In [Christ's] flesh . . . he has abolished the law with its commandments and ordinances, that he might create in himself one new humanity . . . [to] reconcile both groups to God in one body through the cross" (2:14–16).

The element of process is now clear. Salvation is not an event at the end of time but is something taking place in human history. Shifting the metaphor from body to building, the author notes, "In [Christ] the whole structure is joined together and grows into a holy temple in the Lord, in whom you also are built together spiritually into a dwelling place for God" (2:21–22). Returning to the "body" analogy, the author stresses the motif of growth. "We must grow up in every way into him who is the head, into Christ, from whom the whole body, joined and knit together . . . is building itself up in love" (4:15–16). For a cosmic Christ, there is a cosmic church. And, as in Colossians, we have a "realized eschatology." The resurrection is not entirely future. "[God] raised us up with him and seated us with him in the heavenly places in Christ Jesus" (2:6).

4. The Challenge

The threat facing the church is what we have already seen, a disunity brought about by false teachings. "We must no longer be children, tossed to and fro and blown about by every wind of doc-

trine, by people's trickery, by their craftiness in deceitful scheming"
(4:14). So, in Ephesians, unity must be a prime concern for each
Christian, "making every effort to maintain the unity of the Spirit
in the bond of peace" (4:3). What ultimately binds the church
together is made clear. "There is one body and one Spirit . . . one
Lord, one faith, one baptism, one God and Father of all, who is
above all and through all and in all" (4:4–6).

Those exercising leadership in the local churches must contrib-
ute to Christian unity. "The gifts [Christ] gave were that some
would be apostles, some prophets, some evangelists, some pastors
and teachers, to equip the saints for the work of ministry, for building up the body of Christ, until all of us come to the unity of the
faith and of the knowledge of the Son of God, to maturity, to the
measure of the full stature of Christ" (4:11–13). We should note
that in the above passage is the only use of the term "pastor" or
"shepherd" to indicate a church leader in the Pauline letters. When
we recall how vividly the gospel of John depicts Jesus as the "good
shepherd" we might suspect that there is some effort to soften the
rather official titles of "overseer" and "elder." Even today, the
symbol of the bishop is the shepherd's staff or crook.

5. The Orderly Life

Finally, as in Colossians, we have in Ephesians the command
that the Christian lead an orderly and well-regulated life. "Be careful then how you live, not as unwise people but as wise" (5:15).
Again like Colossians, the focus is on the family first. The passage
(Col 3:18–4:1) is expanded in Ephesians (5:22–6:9) with an added
note. " 'For this reason a man will leave his father and mother and
be joined to his wife, and the two will become one flesh.' This is a
great mystery, and I am applying it to Christ and the church"
(5:31–32). We are given another analogy for the profound unity
between Christ and the church—the union of marriage.

We know that Christians differed from both the Jewish and

Gentile cultures in not recognizing divorce, a rule attributed to Christ himself (Mk 10:2–12; Mt 19:3–8; Lk 16:18; also 1 Cor 7:10–11). We do not know the precise circumstances which gave rise to the Christian conviction of the indissolubility of marriage. However, it was so firmly in place that Ephesians could cite it as a model for Christ's union with his church.

But all was not sweetness and light. Ephesians may reflect a growing hostility between the Christians and the world in which they find themselves. "Put on the whole armor of God, so that you may be able to stand against the wiles of the devil. For our struggle is not against enemies of blood and flesh, but against the rulers, against the authorities, against the cosmic powers of this present darkness, against the spiritual forces of evil in the heavenly places" (6:11–12).

The author writes to men and women who live in a world where human destiny was in the control of forces, "principalities and powers" if you will, quite beyond their control. These Christians did not doubt the existence of such "evil spirits"; rather they placed their trust in God to protect them. The Christian is not at the mercy of these forces, armed as he is with truth, justice, the "good news" and faith—all listed as the gear worn by the Roman soldier (6:10–17).

E. SUMMARY

The Pastorals on the one hand, and Colossians with Ephesians on the other, represent two responses to the crisis facing the churches in the sub-apostolic age. Without the authority of the "witnesses" and the founders, how are the integrity of the gospel and the unity of the community to be preserved? The Pastorals met the challenge by stressing the role of an authorized leadership empowered to protect the traditions of the local communities. The authors of Colossians and Ephesians looked beyond the local church to a reality that transcended the local community—a vision of Christ in a living union with the whole church. A Christ of cosmic proportions was guarantor of the fidelity and unity of the Christian community.

These two responses are complimentary, rather than conflicting. We might say that the Pastorals emphasize the external structure of a local hierarchy of offices, headed by the "bishop/elder." Colossians and Ephesians do not deny the role of such local authority, but rather chose to emphasize an internal, invisible, but no less real, protective presence of Christ in his church.

STUDY QUESTIONS

1. To what challenge are the Pastorals a response? What was the response?
2. Who were the Gnostics?
3. What task confronted the "bishop/presbyter" in these Pauline communities?
4. What challenges to the Christian community are reflected in Colossians?
5. In Colossians what change is found in the understanding of the parousia?
6. Is there a new understanding of Christ? Of the church? Of church leadership?
7. What is the cosmic Christ?
8. How does Ephesians depict the church?
9. Why the stress in Ephesians on an orderly life?
10. What model does Ephesians use for the unity of Christ and the church?

VII

The Pauline Communities of the Sub-Apostolic Age: Luke and Acts

A. THE GOSPEL OF LUKE

SUGGESTED READING: LUKE 1:1–2:52; 24:1–50

1. The Author

Luke is not the first to appear of those documents we call gospels. That honor goes to the gospel of Mark. Luke is in fact an extensive rewrite of the earlier work (see Appendix B: The Synoptic Question). Because the gospel of Matthew is similarly dependent on that of Mark, Matthew, Mark and Luke are referred to as the "synoptic" gospels, in that they have the same outline or "synopsis." However, as we shall see, the Lucan tradition is related to Paul and to his communities. Appearing as the gospel does in later years of the first century, Luke gives us a further insight into those communities—hence its being treated at this point.

As with Mark and Matthew, there is no manuscript evidence that indicates the authorship of either Luke or the Acts of the Apostles, the companion work to the gospel. We have second century traditions which attribute the gospel and its companion work to one "Luke" who was a companion of Paul, a conclusion that would seem to be reflected in the so-called "we" passage of Acts (16:10–17; 20:5–15; 21:1–18; 27:1–28:16). However, just who "we" includes other than the apostle is not made clear. A "Luke" is also identified as a companion of Paul in Colossians (4:14), 2 Timothy (4:11) and Philemon (v. 24).

Nevertheless, there remains a serious problem in attributing Luke and Acts to an intimate associate of Paul's. The author of Acts seems curiously unaware of events referred to in Paul's letters. A glaring example can be seen by comparing Galatians (2:1–10) and Acts (15:1–29). Perhaps the simplest solution to such discrepancies is to say that the author of Luke and Acts was actually a companion of Paul's for only those periods represented by the "we" passages; for information covering the other parts of the apostle's career, the author relied on secondary sources. He also was writing some ten to fifteen years after the death of Paul and may have had hazy recollections. However, we can include Luke and Acts in the Pauline tradition and look to them for a further insight into the later development of the Pauline communities.

The author of Luke and Acts is a talented writer of Greek and an excellent stylist. The vividness of his work is testified by the fact that painters, especially those of the renaissance, tend to choose Lucan scenes as their subjects. Luke's Hebrew Bible citations are invariably from the Septuagint, and both Luke and Acts have an overall Hellenistic flavor. Joseph P. Fitzmyer in his *The Gospel According to Luke* concludes, "I regard Luke as a gentile Christian, not, however, as a Greek, but as a non-Jewish Semite, a native of Antioch, where he was well educated in Hellenistic atmosphere and culture" (p. 42). It is generally thought that Luke and Acts were written between 80 and 90 A.D.

2. The Sources

The opening lines of Luke are, "Since many have undertaken to set down an orderly account of the events that have been fulfilled among us, just as they were handed on to us by those who from the beginning were eyewitnesses and servants of the word, I too decided, after investigating everything carefully from the very first, to write an orderly account for you, most excellent Theophilus, so that you may know the truth concerning the things about which you have been instructed" (Lk 1:1–4).

As we see, the author acknowledges the existence of similar works prior to his own. One of these, as mentioned, is the gospel of Mark. Something over fifty percent of Mark is repeated in Luke, and the author uses this material with great freedom, changing the order and adapting it to his own style. He also shares a body of material we find in the gospel of Matthew, the "Q" source (see Appendix B). And, as with Matthew, the author has material unique to himself which we can call the "Lucan tradition," a tradition which is quite different from that of Matthew and Mark.

3. The Lucan Tradition

a. The Infancy Account

One place where the differences between the Matthean and Lucan traditions can be best appreciated is in the two accounts of Jesus' birth. In both traditions the conception of Jesus is the opening event of the "good news"—this in contrast to the gospels of Mark and John where it is Jesus' encounter with John the Baptist. Unfortunately, we tend to coalesce the two "infancy accounts" into one. Mangers, stars, angels, shepherds and magi are all jumbled together in the same crèche. But in doing so, we can fail to see and appreciate the differences between the two depictions of Jesus' birth and the significance of these differences.

The accounts do agree on several points. The parents of Jesus were Mary and Joseph. The conception was remarkable: "The angel said to [Mary], 'The Holy Spirit will come upon you . . . there-

fore the child to be born will be holy; he will be called Son of God' "
(Lk 1:35). "[Mary] was found to be with child from the Holy Spirit"
(Mt 1:18). The place of birth was Bethlehem, and Jesus grew up in
Nazareth. Beyond these points the Lucan and Matthean traditions
are at variance, and the differences give us an insight into their
respective communities.

The opening chapters of Luke consist of a series of beautifully
drawn vignettes that might be titled: "The Announcement of the
Birth of John the Baptist" (1:5ff), "The Announcement of the
Birth of Jesus" (1:26ff), "The Visitation of Mary to Her Cousin
Elizabeth" (1:39ff), and so forth. In the first scene, Zechariah, a
priest, stands in the great temple of Jerusalem. The setting is that of
the old order; as things were before the advent of Jesus. The final
scene of Luke's account has the adolescent Jesus similarly in the
temple, claiming it as his "Father's house" (2:49). Thus the "new"
order has replaced the old.

In Luke, John the Baptist is paralleled with Jesus. Born of aged
parents as was Isaac of Abraham and Sarah, John is a figure that
can be said to represent the Jewish heritage of Luke's community.
In the visitation (1:39ff) Elizabeth, Mary's cousin, greets her on her
arrival, each being pregnant, one with the future Baptist, the other
with the messiah. The scene depicts John's relationship to Jesus;
John's movement in the womb announces the coming of Jesus, just
as the Baptist will do on the banks of the Jordan (3:4–6). Thus, the
"old" prepares the way for the "new."

In both scenes the impression is created that the transition
from Judaism to Christianity was effortless and without tension.
Similarly, figures representing the "old," such as the aged Simeon
(2:29ff) and Anna the prophetess (2:36ff), reminiscent of those
found in the Hebrew Bible, recognize Jesus as "the Lord's Messiah
[the Christ]" (2:26) and as the one promised "to all who were looking for the redemption of Jerusalem" (2:38). Yet we are already
aware of how difficult it was in fact to make that transition. But in

the communities represented by Luke and Acts, it would appear that the bitter controversies now lie in the past and a Gentile Christianity is securely in place.

A further indication of this we can see in a symbol found in the Lucan crèche, one that is easily overlooked. Recounting the circumstances of Jesus' birth, Luke includes the words, "and laid him in a manger" (2:7)—an insignificant detail to us, but Luke's readers, very familiar with the Hebrew Bible, would have immediately recognized the reference to the opening lines of Isaiah: "Hear, O heavens, and listen, O earth; for the Lord has spoken: I reared children and brought them up, but they have rebelled against me. The ox knows its owner, and the donkey its master's crib; but Israel does not know, my people do not understand" (1:2–3). The Lucan community, a *new* people, saw themselves as the new Israel who did understand.

b. From Jewish to Gentile

Thus, it appears that in the Pauline community reflected by Luke's gospel the tensions between Jewish and Gentile Christians have been resolved, perhaps because the membership of the community was now substantially Gentile. Further indication of this is the gospel's omission of the controversies between Jesus and the Pharisees over matters of the law and dietetic restrictions. Luke also omits semitic words and expressions.

In the genealogy of Jesus, his heritage is traced all the way back to Adam, thus relating Jesus to the whole of humankind (3:23–38). This is in contrast to Matthew's very Jewish listing of the Lord's heritage (1:1–16), and echoing Paul's, "There is no longer Jew or Greek, for all of you are one in Christ Jesus" (Gal 3:28)—further evidence of Luke's Gentile bias.

The transition from the Jewish to the Gentile milieus in the Pauline churches is reflected by Luke in another way. In the gospel we are told that Herod is king of Judea (1:5) at the time of John the Baptist's birth. But John, as we have seen, represents the Jewish past. So when we come to the birth of Jesus, the framework is that of the empire: "In those days a decree went out from Emperor Augustus that all the world should be registered. This was the first registration and was taken while Quirinius was governor of Syria" (2:1–2). Jesus' public life is similarly dated: "In the fifteenth year of the reign of Emperor Tiberius" (3:1). We are in the new and Gentile milieu.

c. Concern for Women and Outcasts

We saw earlier in our treatment of the Pauline letters that some conflict existed over the role of women in the church's worship services. It is interesting then to see the role they play in the gospel of Luke, a document we believe stemmed from Pauline communities. For instance, where Joseph is the focus of Matthew's infancy narrative and Mary remains in the background, the exact reverse is true in Luke's account. Further, Luke shows Jesus' concern for women in the treatment of the widow and her son (7:11–15) and the penitent woman (7:36–50). The women in his entourage (8:1–3), Martha and Mary (10:38–42), and the women at the tomb (24:1–11) are all presented as having a role in Jesus' ministry. This could reflect a similar role in the life of the Pauline churches.

It could also indicate the concern these early Christian communities had for the poor and outcast. As is the case in our own times, women of that era often bore the brunt of society's injustice. Such a concern can be seen in other parts of Luke—for example in the Lucan version of the beatitudes (6:20–26), and the narratives concerning the rich fool (12:13–21), the poor at the banquet (14:12–14), and Dives and Lazarus (16:19–31).

We saw earlier Paul's concern for those neglected at the eucharistic banquet (1 Cor 11:21). In 2 Corinthians 8–9, the apostle makes an eloquent plea for generosity to the poor. Poverty, neglect, ostracism and similar evils were as much a part of the ancient world as they are of ours. Paul's concern for the victims, the outcasts, is shared by the author of Luke and by the Pauline communities for which he wrote.

B. THE ACTS OF THE APOSTLES

SUGGESTED READINGS: ACTS 1:1–2:47

1. The Transition

Acts relates, in an idealized manner, the movement of Christianity from its Jewish to its Gentile milieu, principally in the relating of the career of Paul, "the apostle to the Gentiles." Yet the pioneer in this process is not Paul, but Peter, as we read in the account of Peter's meeting with the centurion Cornelius (10:1–48). Peter's remark, "I truly understand that God shows no partiality, but in every nation anyone who fears him and does what is right is acceptable to him" (10:34–35), could have been said by Paul. It was also Peter who had the vision that challenged the Jewish dietary laws (11:1–10) which allowed him to eat with the "uncircumcised," Paul in Galatians (2:11ff) to the contrary. Further, at the meeting in Jerusalem as pictured in Acts (15:1ff), it is Peter who defends Paul's position on circumcision, and James, the head of the Jerusalem church, who proposes the compromise solution. As in the gospel, the transition is without tension or serious conflict.

2. The Role of the Spirit

a. The Meaning of Spirit

Even the most cursory reading of Paul's letters would reveal the central role in the life of the churches and of the Christians played by the "Spirit." However, care must be taken not to read into these references an understanding of the terms "Holy Spirit" or "Spirit of God" that the church will not arrive at for another two centuries. The Greek word "pneuma" and the Hebrew "ruah" have the same meaning—"breath." In the Hebrew Bible, "ruah" is the principle of life. We find in Genesis, "The Lord God formed

156   EXPLORING SCRIPTURE

man from the dust of the ground, and breathed into his nostrils the
breath of life; and the man became a living being" (2:7). "Ruah"
also means "wind" whose force and direction can have such a
dramatic effect on the climate of the Middle East. Thus in ancient
times the wind was called the "ruah" of God. The "Spirit of God"
in the Hebrew Bible is a way of speaking of God's power.

   b. *The Role of the Spirit in the Church*

   In the gospel of Luke, the story of Jesus begins with the Spirit:
"The Holy Spirit will come upon you" (1:35) are the words of the
angel to Mary. Similarly, the story of the church will begin with the
Spirit. At his ascension, Jesus tells his followers, "You will receive
power when the Holy Spirit has come upon you; and you will be
my witnesses in Jerusalem, in all Judea and Samaria, and to the
ends of the earth" (Acts 1:8). The promise is fulfilled in the events
of Pentecost.

   Fifty days after Passover, the Jews celebrated (as they do today) the giving of the law to Moses on Mount Sinai "wrapped in
smoke, because the Lord had descended upon it in fire" (Ex 19:18).
It is on that feast day, Pentecost, that Acts tells of the coming of the
Spirit upon the church and in a manner reminding the reader of the
scene at Sinai. "And suddenly from heaven there came a sound like
the rush of a violent wind. . . . Divided tongues, as of fire, appeared
among them, and a tongue rested on each of them. All of them were
filled with the Holy Spirit" (2:2–4). In the scene that follows, people
from every part of the Roman world hear Peter, the leader of the
"witnesses," preach the "good news," each "in our own language"
(2:11). Certainly, such unity of language is meant to remind the
reader of the scene at the foot of the tower of Babel (Gen 12:9). The
disunity of humankind, symbolized by that "babble," is now to be
healed by the unifying spread of the "good news." We have here, in
microcosm, how the Lucan churches must have envisioned themselves as the first century ended.

   c. *The Leadership and the Spirit*

   The "sub-apostolic" pastoral letters indicated the development of an authoritative leadership. In Acts we read, "they had

appointed elders for them in each church" (14:23). Later, "[Paul] sent a message to Ephesus, asking the elders of the church to meet him. When they came to him, he said to them: 'Keep watch over yourselves and over all the flock, of which the Holy Spirit has made you overseers, to shepherd the church of God' " (20:17–18,28). Here again is a leadership that is to "oversee" the Pauline churches, authorized to do so by "the Spirit of God." Is there a broader mandate for church leadership? Peter and "the eleven" (2:14) in the Pentecost scene reflect the role of the leadership in these late first century Christian communities.

3. Summary

The Pauline communities about which we first read in Luke and Acts had long been separated from the Jewish synagogues, a transition that appears to have been made without the rancor and bitterness that characterized other churches. At the end of the apostolic age and with the departure of the "witnesses," the Pauline communities had placed church leadership in the hands of the presbyter/elders who had the responsibility of protecting the traditions from deviant variations. The leadership had also to maintain the unity of the churches. The Pauline communities came to a broader understanding of church as transcending the local communities, a church in which Christ himself was present. In all of this, and inspired certainly by Paul's preaching and writing, these churches came to a profound appreciation of God's constant care and "inspiration." The "Spirit" was a way they spoke of this continuing presence.

STUDY QUESTIONS

1. What can we surmise about the author of Luke and Acts?
2. What are the sources of the gospel?

3. On what points in their infancy accounts do Matthew and Luke agree?
4. What indications do we find in Luke's opening chapters that indicate an end to the Jewish/Gentile conflict in the Pauline communities?
5. What other concerns are expressed in the Lucan tradition?
6. What role does the Spirit play in the Pauline communities for which Luke and Acts were written?
7. What indications are there in Luke and Acts of the leadership in the Pauline communities? How is this reflected in the Pentecost scene?

VIII

The Christian Community
in Rome

A. THE BEGINNINGS

As with all the large urban areas of the empire, Rome had its colony of Jews. They were there in goodly numbers by the middle of the second century B.C., and as time passed they gained an increasing influence which occasionally resulted in a rise of anti-semitism. However the Jews supported Julius Caesar and had the good fortune to be on the winning side of the struggles that followed his demise. The Jews were accorded special privileges, such as free-dom of assembly and exemption from military service, and it was recognized that they could not be compelled to participate in the pagan rituals. The Jewish community could also send contribu-tions out of the country for the support of the temple. The Jews of Rome were particularly devoted to Jerusalem and its religious leadership.

Suetonius, the Roman historian, tells of an edict issued by Emperor Claudius ordering the expulsion of the Jews from Rome due to disturbances over a certain "Chrestus." If this is a misspell-ing of "Christus," as many believe it is, then we can assume a presence of Christians in the imperial capital earlier than 49 A.D., the date of Claudius' death. The Acts of the Apostles refers to this edict (18:2) when Paul, arriving in Corinth in 50 or 51 A.D., meets Aquila and Priscilla. They had just come from Rome as a result of the expulsion of Jews.

It was said, "All roads lead to Rome," so it would not have been long after the time of Jesus that some of his followers reached the center of the empire and became part of the thriving Jewish community there. They would have found it well organized with a number of synagogues whose membership included many influential figures in Roman public life. As long as the Christians were regarded as Jews, they enjoyed the privileges accorded the Jewish community.

B. PAUL'S LETTER TO ROME

SUGGESTED READING: THE LETTER TO THE ROMANS

When Paul was in Corinth again in 58 A.D. he planned to visit Rome, and he took the occasion to write a letter to the Christian community there. As he was unknown to the members of that community, the letter is by way of introduction. Paul, however, was hardly uninformed about the Roman Christian community. His associates Aquila and Priscilla would have been one source of his information. At the end of his letter to Rome (Rom 16:3ff) Paul sends personal greetings to a whole list of acquaintances, leading off with his old friends, Aquila and Priscilla (here called Prisca). This community welcomed him when he arrived in Rome in 61 A.D. (Acts 28:11–30). Tradition has it that the Christian community witnessed his martyrdom several years later.

It would appear from the letter that the Christian community in the capital was predominantly Gentile, but there must have been a sizable minority of Jewish converts in their midst. The general Jewish community of Rome, at the time, was under the influence of their religious center in Jerusalem. Similarly, the Christian community (still seen as a sect of Judaism) related more directly to the churches of Judea under the aegis of Peter and James. Paul and his more liberal communities would have been regarded with suspicion by the Roman Christians. Assuaging that fear was one purpose of the Pauline letter.

Paul may have had another motive in writing to the Roman church. Leaving Corinth in 57 A.D. Paul was to journey to Jerusalem carrying a collection for the benefit of the poor Christians in Judea. He hoped for a friendly reception by the mother-church of Christianity. However, if the positions he expressed in Galatians (see above) about the respective roles of "faith" and "law" had reached the leadership of the Jerusalem church, he would have faced problems there. Romans, which takes a more moderate view of Jewish/Gentile relations, could have been Paul's attempt to win the support of this most influential church in the empire's capital as he headed for the holy city of both Judaism and Christianity.

Thus when Paul speaks in Romans of Abraham as an example of faith (4:1ff) and says also, "Do we then overthrow the law by this faith? By no means! On the contrary, we uphold the law" (3:31), we can conclude that his readers maintained a strong attachment to their Jewish heritage. Paul certainly softens the rhetoric he used earlier in a more polarized circumstance, hoping to create a more favorable impression on the Roman community.

Romans also indicates that some of the Roman Christians were still complying with the more moderate dietetic restrictions of Judaism, probably taking a conservative position on the eating of meat that had been used in pagan sacrificial rituals. Paul does not mete out condemnation, but calls for tolerance. "Those who eat must not despise those who abstain, and those who abstain must not pass judgment on those who eat" (14:3). The church in Rome was far from homogeneous; its members followed differing lifestyles.

In Galatians (2:11–14), Paul admonished Peter for his conservative conduct in separating himself from the Gentile converts. Romans, in contrast, puts the burden on the liberal position. "It is good not to eat meat or drink wine or do anything that makes your brother or sister stumble" (14:21). Again, Paul shows a sensitivity to the moderate members of Rome's church while attesting to the presence of a more liberal group in the community. Some feel that the conservative character of the Christian community in Rome resulted from the influence of Peter and the leadership in Jerusalem.

C. THE GOSPEL OF MARK

SUGGESTED READING: THE GOSPEL OF MARK

1. The Author

"The beginning of the good news of Jesus Christ, the Son of God" (Mk 1:1). These are the opening words of a document written, it is generally agreed, prior to the events of 70 A.D. (see Appendix B). As the document is not signed we must rely on later traditions and on internal evidence to draw our conclusions as to the author, his sources in the oral tradition and his audience. Raymond Brown makes the following observation: "If we put together all of the connections we have seen, it seems likely that *by the early second century a tradition was in circulation that Mark,* presumably John *Mark* of Jerusalem, who had traveled with Paul in the '40s and who had been a companion of Peter and Paul in Rome in the '60s, *wrote a gospel at Rome under the influence of Peter* just before or shortly after Peter's death [which took place no later than 67]. . . . Rome as the site [of composition] cannot be quickly dismissed as implausible" (*Antioch & Rome,* pp. 194, 197; Brown's emphasis). In view of this conclusion, what does Mark tell us of his community?

2. The Failure of the Leaders

A decisive point comes in Mark with a dialogue between Jesus and his disciples when he asks them, "Who do people say that I am?" (8:27). At their response "John the Baptist . . . Elijah . . . one of the prophets" (8:28), Jesus continues, "But who do you say that I am?" It is Peter who responds, "You are the Messiah!" (8:29). But immediately Peter reveals his failure to understand the implications of that title, "that the Son of Man must undergo great suffering, and be rejected by the elders, the chief priests, and the scribes, and be killed" (8:31). Jesus harshly rebukes Peter, "Get behind me, Satan! For you are setting your mind not on divine things but on human things" (8:33). These words are addressed to the one regarded as the leader of the apostles and one whom the churches, especially Rome, held in the highest regard. But there is more.

On the second occasion when Jesus reveals what is to be his fate (9:30ff), his disciples again fail to grasp the meaning of his words and proceed to argue over who will hold the highest rank in the coming "kingdom," obviously seen by them as a "this worldly" power. Finally, as Jesus and his disciples approach Jerusalem on the eve of the climactic events his life, Jesus reiterates for the third time what is about to happen (10:32ff). Oblivious to what has just been said, James and John approach Jesus asking for the highest positions in his glorious realm. Thus both Peter and the Lord's most intimate associates, his disciples, are shown to be uncomprehending and insensitive to Jesus' pronouncements on his impending trials and death (10:33–34).

3. The Meaning of the Passion

The gospel of Mark can be described as a passion narrative with an introduction. The final events of Jesus' life occupy a proportionally larger space in Mark than in the other gospels. The account of Jesus' death was most likely the earliest part of the Christian tradition to become fixed in its outline. The seven day, Sunday to Sunday framework, preserved in all the gospels, reflects a primitive, week-long memorial celebration. It was this early tradition that the gospel of Mark expands upon.

Also, the oldest manuscripts we have of Mark conclude with the discovery of the empty tomb by a group of women who are told of the raising of Jesus and are instructed to inform his disciples (16:1–8). In failing to recount an appearance of the resurrected Christ, Mark heightens the emphasis on the passion, though it should be noted that some scholars hold these manuscripts to be defective, and current editions of the New Testament usually include three ancient attempts to "fill in the gap," none of which are by the author of the gospel.

Given the central and crucial role of the passion, why does Mark show the most revered leader of the church, Peter, and the figures that represented the Jerusalem community, James and John, as well as the rest of the disciples to be insensitive to the central role of the passion of Jesus? In fact, the only one in Mark who knows the true identity of Jesus is a Gentile who has seen none of Jesus' miracles and did not see the risen Christ. He makes his "act of faith" at the foot of the cross. "Now when the centurion, who stood facing him, saw that in this way he breathed his last, he said, 'Truly this man was God's Son!' " (15:39). More to our point, does this severe criticism of the church leadership tell us something about the Christian community in Rome just prior to 70 A.D.?

4. The Tragedy

In July of 64 A.D. a fire destroyed a major portion of Rome. Emperor Nero took the opportunity to begin an ambitious program of urban renewal, giving rise to the suspicion that the fire was started at his behest to facilitate such a renewal. As Tacitus (*Annals* 15:44) tells it, "To suppress this rumor Nero created scapegoats. He punished with every refinement of cruelty the notoriously depraved group which were popularly called Christians." So cruel was this persecution that it actually gave rise to a feeling of pity on the part of the general population of the city for the victims. It is possible that both Peter and Paul died as a result of this tragedy.

It is also possible that in the light of this disaster, the author of

Mark felt that the Christian leadership and perhaps the Christian community itself had failed to anticipate or understand what had happened to them. Were they were too focused on an anticipated glorious return of the risen Christ (the parousia), too confident of victory to be prepared for defeat? In Mark Jesus makes clear the role that suffering must play in the life of his disciples, "If any want to become my followers, let them deny themselves and take up their cross and follow me" (8:34). This would explain Mark's focus on the Lord's passion.

Returning to the gospel of Luke for a moment, we saw how sensitive the Pauline communities were to the role of leadership, so we are not surprised that Luke omits the condemnation of Peter (9:18–22) in the passage that parallels Mark (8:27ff) and makes no mention of the request of James and John for the highest places in the "kingdom" (Mk 10:35ff). In general the disciples of Jesus are seen in a much more favorable light in the gospel of Luke than in that of Mark. As we shall see later, Matthew similarly corrects the picture of church leadership we find in Mark.

5. The Gentile Church

In one aspect in particular, the gospel of Mark gives us a different picture of a Christian community from the one presented in Paul's letter to the church in Rome. In Romans, Paul writes to a church with strong ties to its Jewish heritage. The apostle must handle the question of observance of the "law" in a much more cautious manner than he does in Galatians. In contrast, the author of Mark must explain Jewish customs (7:3–4)—rather odd for the community to which Paul wrote. Similarly, would Paul's Roman community have tolerated such a picture as Mark gives of the revered leader, Peter, and of the figures closely associated with Jesus, James, John and the rest of the disciples, especially in light of the tradition that Peter died a martyr? Could something have happened in the intervening decade between Paul's letter and the gospel of Mark that would explain such a change?

One thing we know occurred—the outbreak of the Jewish war in 66 A.D. It was a particularly vicious rebellion in which the Roman legions were led by two of the emperors that followed the reign of Nero, an event that certainly did nothing to enhance the status of things Jewish in the capital of the empire. The author of Mark might well have stressed the Gentile character of the church to avoid the odium that was attached to it in Rome as a Jewish sect.

Would this also be, in part, the reason for putting the "Jewish" leadership of the church, Peter and the disciples, in a poor light where it is a centurion, a Roman soldier, who expresses the Christian's faith in Jesus? Similarly, the Roman procurator, Pontius Pilate, is depicted as reluctant to execute Jesus and seeks to avoid doing so by offering to free Jesus instead of the rebel and murderer Barabbas. Knowing what we know of Pilate, such a reluctance would be most uncharacteristic. It is also possible that the Roman church did, in the intervening period, gain sufficient Gentile membership to make the community less Jewish in character.

In any event, the gospel of Mark must have gained wide circulation among the Christian communities at the end of the first century. We have already seen its influence on Luke, and we shall also see that it will form the framework on which Matthew writes his gospel. However, we have now to consider two other documents that are traditionally related to the Roman Christian community.

D. THE FIRST LETTER OF PETER

SUGGESTED READING: 1 PETER

It is generally agreed that 1 Peter was written from Rome sometime in the 80s (Raymond Brown, *Antioch & Rome,* p. 128). The capital city is referred to as "Babylon" (5:13), an appropriate appellation subsequent to the destruction of Jerusalem and its great temple. The date precludes the chief apostle from being the author, in spite of the opening words, "Peter, an apostle of Jesus

Christ . . ." (1:1). The letter appears to have been addressed to moderately conservative Christians in the mideast. These could have been communities evangelized by Peter, which remained faithful to that apostle's views—hence the adoption of his name by the unknown author.

Our interest here is not in what 1 Peter tells us about the receiving Christian communities but about the community of the author which we can assume would be a similarly moderate group in the Roman church. Their "Jewishness" is reflected in the use of Hebrew Bible motifs in 1 Peter and an appeal to that heritage. "But you are 'a chosen race, a royal priesthood, a holy nation, God's own people' " (2:9)—all titles of ancient Israel.

Besides showing us the continued influence of the Roman community's roots, 1 Peter also indicates that the church in the capital had taken on some of the structural elements we saw in the Pastorals. "Now as an elder myself I . . . exhort the elders among you to tend the flock of God that is in your charge, exercising the oversight [episkopeo], not under compulsion but willingly" (5:1–2). The Roman church had confronted the departure of the "witnesses," as had the other sub-apostolic churches, by accepting an authoritative leadership in order to preserve their traditions. In spite of what we saw in Mark, the respect for their Jewish heritage and leadership remained present in the Roman Christian community.

E. THE LETTER TO THE HEBREWS

SUGGESTED READING: HEBREWS

The letter to the Hebrews was for a time attributed to the apostle Paul, probably due to the reference to Paul's companion, Timothy, which is found in its closing lines (12:23). Rejection of this attribution is about the only thing modern scripture scholarship agrees on concerning Hebrews. The date of composition is

80–90 A.D., and thus the letter is sub-apostolic. Everything points to its author being a Hellenized Jewish Christian, familiar with the Greek language and culture. Apollos, mentioned in both Acts and in Paul's authentic writings (see above), is suggested by some to be the author.

Though Hebrews is referred to as a letter, it is more of a treatise addressed to a group of Christian converts from Judaism who, out of nostalgia, were being drawn to return to their original convictions. The letter is a gentle polemic against such a move. Hebrews focuses on the ritual life of the Jew, but stressing that Jesus is greater than Moses (3:3ff) and is a superior high priest (4:14ff). Jesus "is the mediator of a better covenant, which has been enacted through better promises" (8:6), and is "the greater and perfect tent (temple)" (9:11). Finally, Jesus' sacrifice eliminates the need for any other (10:10ff).

Raymond Brown argues at length for the possibility that the document was destined for the Christian community in Rome (*Antioch & Rome,* pp. 142–49). We have commented on the attachment that the Roman church had for the Jerusalem community and things Jewish in our discussion above of Romans and 1 Peter. For this reason, many of Rome's Christians would have felt most acutely the disaster of 70 A.D. and the destruction of the Jewish center of worship. Hebrews could be seen as an antidote to nostalgia for this destroyed past and any attempt to preserve some of it in Christian life and worship. We are reminded again that the Jewish wars culminated in a tragedy for both Jew and Christian.

We can easily imagine the anguish the Roman Christians must have undergone as the triumphal march of Titus' legions made its way through the capital city amid a cheering populace. As depicted in the arch commemorating the emperor's victory, these Christians saw in the hands of the conquerors the loot taken from Jerusalem's great temple, clear evidence of that marvel's destruction. For a community with strong ties to a Jewish heritage, the scene before them must have been painful indeed. It must also have brought home to them forcibly that the church's future lay in the Gentile

world. Having undergone persecution under the emperor's predecessor, Nero, these Christians must have been aware how tenuous
was that future.

F. SUMMARY

In the centuries to come, the church in Rome took on an ever
greater importance, but we must not read that future into the past.
It was probably the Christian community in Jerusalem that exerted
the most influence until the city's destruction in 70 A.D. The community in Antioch, which we shall discuss next, was also very prestigious. However, even in the earliest days, the Roman church must
have been significant; witness Paul's desire to visit that Christian
community. Also four New Testament documents (the largest
number) are associated with it, and both Peter and Paul are traditionally said to have died in Rome, martyrs for their faith.

The Christian community had its roots in the Jewish community, though there was conflict between the two very early on, as we
saw from the expulsion of both groups from the city. The strong
attachment of the Christian church to its Jewish heritage is attested
to by Paul's letter to that community. But a decade later, when the
gospel of Mark was written, we find that a profound change had
taken place, very possibly resulting from the outbreak of a rebellion
of Jewish extremists in Palestine. The strong Gentile flavor of the
gospel may represent an effort to escape a Jewish past. The gospel
also reveals a disenchantment with the church's leadership which
appears to have failed to understand the role of the passion of Jesus
in the work of salvation.

The first letter of Peter and the letter to the Hebrews, coming
late in the first century, indicate something of a return to an appreciation of the Jewish roots of Christianity and an emphasis on the
importance of leadership in the church. It is likely that the community in Rome was facing the challenge we saw in the Pauline
churches where the integrity of tradition had to be preserved from

deviant challenges. At this point, the New Testament record of the Roman church ends.

STUDY QUESTIONS

1. What was the first known reference to Christians in Rome?
2. What reasons would Paul have had for writing to the Christian community in Rome?
3. What are the differences between what Paul wrote to the Galatians and what he wrote to Rome?
4. What picture does Mark give us of the church's leadership and what might this indicate?
5. Why does Mark stress the suffering and death of Jesus and apparently downplay the resurrection?
6. What group of Roman Christians is reflected in 1 Peter? What are the indications of this?
7. What appears to be the purpose of Hebrews?

IX

Matthew's Gospel and the Antioch Community

A. ANTIOCH AND THE COMING OF CHRISTIANITY

1. The City

As we have already noted, Mark's gospel proved to be the most prestigious document since circulated among the sub-apostolic Christian communities of the first century, probably not long after the disaster of 70 A.D. It made its influence felt in the Pauline communities as we saw in our discussion of Luke's gospel, and at the same time it must have come to the attention of the Christians in Antioch.

Already three hundred years old by the time of Jesus, Antioch was the third most important city in the empire. Its population approached one million, and the city was Hellenistic in culture, as well as cosmopolitan and ethnically diverse. Included in the population of Antioch was a large colony of Jews. They were a prosperous, well organized community and enjoyed privileges not accorded other groups. The Romans, after their conquests in the 60s B.C., designated the city as the capital of the province of Syria.

2. The Christians

Among the Jews of the city was a growing sect which had accepted Jesus of Nazareth as the messiah. As we are told in Acts

(11:19–20) members of this group, fleeing from persecution in Jerusalem, came to Antioch sometime in the 30s A.D. "It was in Antioch that the disciples were first called 'Christians' " (11:26). In the beginning the Christians were associated with the Jewish community, making converts among them to "the way" (9:2). However, after a time, an appeal was also made to the Gentiles, who, much to everyone's surprise, responded in considerable numbers. Seeing this, the Jerusalem church sent Barnabas to inquire into the matter (11:22), and, as we saw above, he in turn went to Tarsus and summoned Paul (11:25–26). After this team was successful in Antioch, Paul and Barnabas were sent by that community on the first of the apostle's missionary journeys (13:2–3).

3. The Controversy

On their return, a dispute broke out about which we have seen a great deal in Paul's life and letters. It stemmed from his liberal policy of allowing Gentiles to enter the Christian community without circumcision and, at best, a limited adherence to the law, particularly the dietetic code. The crucial moment is described variously in Galatians (2:1ff) and Acts (15:1ff). At a Jerusalem meeting, the leadership of the mother church settled the question in Paul's favor. Later however, in Antioch, Peter backed away from this liberal policy under pressure from members of the Jerusalem church.

After this, Paul seems to have lost out to Peter as a dominant influence over the Antiochean church. Save for the incident in Galatians, Paul never mentions his "home base" in his letters. The apostle's interest is confined to those churches of which he was the founder, Rome being the one exception. One is left with the impression that the Antiochean community, however liberal it might have been under the influence of Paul, retreated from his position. Later, the city's Christian church appeared to be made up of a right wing composed of Jews and even Gentiles who complied with the full Jewish code, including circumcision, and a moderately conservative group, possibly Petrine in character. These were Jews and Gentiles who complied with Jewish dietary regulations but did not demand that the Gentile converts be circumcised. Finally, there was a small liberal group of Christians that did not require any compliance with the Jewish code and represented the remaining Pauline influence. With the outbreak of the Jewish wars (63–67 A.D.) and the disaster of 70 A.D., the Christian community in the Syrian capital was radically altered.

4. The Disaster of 70 A.D.

We have already seen the traumatic effects of the destruction of Jerusalem and its great temple on the Christian community in Rome. That shock must have been immensely greater in a city so much closer to what had been the very heart of Judaism. The Jewish religion was radically changed, and, in an effort to preserve its traditions, the Pharisaic sect became dominant and demanded conformity in the Jewish synagogues. Deviations were not tolerated, leading to the expulsion of those Christians who were still maintaining their connections with Judaism.

The resultant bitterness can be seen in Matthew's gospel where we read, "they will flog you in their synagogues" (10:17). The identification of Christianity as a non-Jewish group certainly gained momentum and brought with it other difficulties. "They will hand you over to councils . . . you will be dragged before governors and kings" (10:17–18). The predominantly Gentile churches would have been only marginally affected by these changes; not so the Christians in Antioch with their strong attachment to their Jewish heritage.

The tragedy of 70 A.D. destroyed the Jerusalem Christian community, the mother church. And no Christian community was more affected by this than the church in Antioch which had always had a close relationship with the source community. The Antiochean Christians were cut off from their roots. As John Meier puts it,

"They were now adrift in a Gentile sea, headed for a Gentile future" (*Antioch & Rome*, p. 49). The manner in which that future was faced by these Christians is reflected in Matthew's gospel.

B. THE GOSPEL AND ITS SOURCES

SUGGESTED READING: THE GOSPEL OF MATTHEW, CHAPTERS 1, 2, 5, 16 AND 27

1. The Author

Within fifteen or twenty years of Jerusalem's destruction, Matthew's gospel makes its appearance. As with Mark and Luke, no name is found on the earliest manuscripts. A second century tradition attests to a gospel written in Aramaic by the apostle Matthew in the early 60s A.D. There is no way of knowing whether such a document ever existed. The gospel we attribute to Matthew gives no evidence of being a translation of an earlier Aramaic work. Rather, it appears to have been originally written in Greek. The gospel makes use of the Greek translation of the Hebrew Bible (the Septuagint) and quotes Mark extensively (see Appendix B), also written in Greek. The author gives every evidence of being a Jewish Christian, quite possibly a former scribe. The place of origin cannot be known exactly, but the church in Antioch reflects much of what we can surmise about the Christian community for which Matthew was written.

2. The Community of the Gospel

Since Matthew, in spite of being generally Hellenistic in character, has a strong Jewish flavor, we can conclude that his was a community with strong ties to that culture and religion. The author's interest in Jesus' relationship to the scribes and Pharisees is greater than that found in the other gospels. Matthew also has a more detailed description of Jewish laws and customs and places greater stress on Jesus' mission to the people of Israel: "Go nowhere among the Gentiles . . . go rather to the lost sheep of the house of Israel" (10:5–6). "I was sent only to the lost sheep of the house of Israel" (15:24).

On the other hand, the command to evangelize the Gentile world is clearly stated in Jesus' final words to his apostles: "Go therefore and make disciples of all nations" (28:19). Matthew also shows Gentiles in a favorable light at several points. There is the centurion who requests the cure of his paralyzed servant (8:5ff) and the Canaanite woman begging for the cure of her daughter (15:21ff), both being praised for their faith. We should note that Mark's Gentile centurion, standing at the foot of the cross, is now joined by his men in proclaiming, "Truly this man was God's Son!" (Mt 27:54). A Christian community with a complex relationship between Jewish and Gentile memberships would seem to fit Antioch quite accurately. As we examine Matthew in greater detail, the evidence that Antioch is its city of origin will become even stronger.

3. The Matthean Tradition

Matthew regards Mark so highly that the author reuses 600 of the 660 verses found in the earlier gospel. Matthew shares with Luke the source called "Q" (see Appendix B). The remaining material represents the Matthean tradition. Considerable insight into the makeup of Matthew's church can be gained from an examination of those parts unique to his gospel. As we saw above, the church's mission to both Jew and Gentile is reflected in the Matthean tradition.

We can also see an interplay between the more conservative and the less conservative members of Matthew's community in the "sermon on the mount" (5:3–44). In these passages the prescriptions of the law are not rescinded, but given a greater moral force. "Do not think that I have come to abolish the law or the prophets; I have come not to abolish but to fulfill" (5:17). So changed, this "new" law would say to the Gentiles that though they are freed from the strictures of the "old" law, they are nevertheless bound to a stricter moral code. The expression "You have heard that it was said . . ." is followed by, "But I say to you . . ." This pattern is repeated several times (5:21, 27, 33, 38, 43); each time Jesus calls his hearers to a higher ethic. By taking such a position, Matthew allays the fears of the more conservative membership that the influx of Gentiles would in effect weaken the morals of the church.

Balancing the influence of the liberal and Gentile elements in the community with those of the conservative and Jewish is a concern that governed the formation of Matthew's gospel in many ways—something we will see more of as we continue our discussion of the author's distinctive tradition.

4. Leadership in Matthew's Church

As we have seen, the trauma of being severed from their roots in Judaism and from the synagogue affected the Matthean Christians most acutely. Without the guidance of the Jerusalem church, the role of leadership in the local community would have become crucial. In the apostle's letters and in Luke we saw how an authoritative leadership evolved in the Pauline communities. The gospel of Mark showed a similar development in the Roman church. However, unlike the letters, these gospels, as well as that of John, do not use the term "church." The authors of Mark, Luke and John recognize that the term would be out of place in the mouth of Jesus, since the Christian communities came into existence after his death and resurrection.

It is Matthew alone who uses the term "church," and then only on two occasions. Jesus tells his disciples that the church is to be the final arbiter in disputes among the members (18:15ff). The exercise of this authority (the meaning of "to bind and loose") is ratified by the highest power. "Truly I tell you, whatever you bind on earth will be bound in heaven, and whatever you loose on earth will be loosed in heaven" (18:18).

The other use of "church" in Matthew is in one of the most discussed passages in Matthew, if not in all the gospels. It occurs where Matthew parallels Mark. Peter responds to Jesus' query "But who do you say that I am?" with "You are the Messiah!" (Mk 8:29; Mt 16:15). But Peter fails to understand the meaning of his answer. For this he is severely admonished, "Get behind me, Satan! You are a stumbling block to me; for you are setting your mind not on divine things but on human things" (Mk 8:33; Mt 16:23). The author of Luke, as we saw, simply ignored the admonition of Peter (9:18ff). Matthew, however, makes some most significant additions to the Markan passage—changes aimed at strengthening the role of leadership in the community, a role that could have been weakened by Mark's criticism.

First of all, Peter's reply is made more complete: "You are the Messiah, the Son of the living God" (16:16). In between Peter's answer and his failure to understand, the author inserts, "Blessed are you, Simon son of Jonah! For flesh and blood has not revealed this to you, but my Father in heaven. And I tell you, you are Peter, and on this rock I will build my church . . . I will give you the keys of the kingdom of heaven, and whatever you bind on earth will be bound in heaven, and whatever you loose on earth will be loosed in heaven" (16:17–19). The authority given to the community (18:18) is entrusted to the leader of the apostles. John Meier points out: "Matthew is presenting Peter as the chief Rabbi of the universal church, with power to make 'halakic' decisions (i.e. decisions on conduct) in the light of the teachings of Jesus" (op. cit. pp. 66–67).

As Peter was certainly deceased when the gospel was written, we can assume that the Petrine authority persisted in the Matthean community. This "rehabilitation" is extended to the rest of the apostles as well. After Jesus' second prophecy of his passion, the apostles do not fail to understand, as they do in Mark (9:32), but are "greatly distressed" in Matthew (17:23). After the third prediction of the passion, Mark has James and John, the sons of Zebedee, approach Jesus with a request to occupy the seats of honor in the new kingdom (10:35ff)—again, a failure to understand. In Matthew the request is not made by the two apostles directly, but by their mother (20:20). Matthew is careful to soften the criticism of church leadership that we find in Mark. In doing this, the author is reflecting the role that an authoritative leadership must have played in Matthew's church.

We can probably presume that Matthew reflected the situation in his community during the sub-apostolic age which must have faced the same challenges that confronted the Pauline churches and the church in Rome. These local churches were without the protective influence once exercised by Jerusalem and the "witnesses" which protected them from deviant traditions. Though it could be criticized as is evidenced in Mark, the role of church leadership was recognized as essential.

In the case of the Antiochean church this role becomes quite clear at the beginning of the second century. In a series of letters written between 108 and 117 A.D. by Ignatius of Antioch, "we find a clearly delineated three-tier hierarchy of one bishop, a group of presbyters, and a group of deacons. Clearly the bishop is *the* leader. . . . The bishop is also the chief teacher in the church, guaranteeing the unity of faith and the unity of the church" (John P. Meier, op. cit. p. 74). Ignatius was himself the bishop of Antioch—perhaps the first—being martyred during the reign of Trajan (98–117 A.D.). If Matthew originated in Antioch around 85 A.D., then within fifteen years what we can infer about the church's leadership from the gospel becomes a full-blown reality.

5. The New for the Old

We have spoken of the transitions reflected in Matthew as the church in Antioch moved into the sub-apostolic age. Severed from the foundational community in Jerusalem, the community moved from a Jewish to a Gentile membership and became less attached to the "old" law and its restrictions, finally developing an authoritative leadership to replace the "witnesses." An addition that Matthew makes to a passage in Mark throws more light on what we have been saying. In Mark we have, "And no one puts new wine into old wineskins; otherwise, the wine will burst the skins, and the wine is lost, and so are the skins; but one puts new wine into fresh wineskins" (2:22). Matthew repeats the passage but continues, "so both [wine and skins] are preserved" (9:17). Mark shows no concern for the fate of the "old skins," i.e. Judaism, since his gospel shows little concrete interest in Judaism. Matthew, given his church's heritage, must take care in preserving the "old skins," and so his gospel does.

We can see how Matthew's community safeguarded its Jewish traditions in the role played by the prophecies quoted from the Hebrew Bible. For almost every event in the gospel narrative, the author of Matthew supplies the reader with a Hebrew Bible citation; the "old" is the key to understanding the "new." Nowhere is the delicate relationship between the "old" and the "new" clearer than in the "infancy" narrative, a section unique to Matthew.

6. The Infancy Account

The gospel of Luke showed us a Christian community that made the transition from Jewish to Gentile with apparent ease. It was respectful of its Jewish heritage, but you have the impression that Judaism is very much something of the past. In contrast, the Jewish heritage of Matthew's church is something quite immediate. For instance, by tracing the genealogy of Jesus back to Adam (3:23ff), Luke relates the Nazarene to all of humankind. Matthew, however, in the opening passage of his gospel (1:ff), begins with the patriarch Abraham in tracing the "family record of Jesus Christ" down through the kings of Judah to "Joseph the husband of Mary."

It was to this "upright" Jew (1:18–25) who was deeply concerned about the law that the birth of the messiah was announced. He is a Judean residing with his wife in Bethlehem, the city of David, as against Luke where the couple are Nazarenes. It is in Matthew's account of Jesus' birth that we can see most clearly the role of the Jewish heritage in the church of Antioch.

Forget for a moment the Lucan crèche with its manger, angels and shepherds. The astrologers (magi) are the key to the meaning of Matthew's Christmas story (2:1–12). They are Gentiles guided by the "star" which symbolizes their wisdom, astrology. Astrology incidentally enjoyed a respect in the ancient world as a science that it does not generally have today. The "star," however, did not provide sufficient guidance, and on their arrival in Jerusalem the magi had to consult the Jewish civil and religious leadership.

The irony would not be lost on Matthew's readers. The Jews, drawing on their "wisdom," their knowledge of the Hebrew Bible, gave correct directions to the Magi—directions they themselves were not willing to follow. The "star" and the lore of the Hebrew Bible together guide the magi on the final leg of their journey. After presenting their gifts, symbolic of their presence in the church, to the child, the magi are given further divine guidance which protects the safety of the infant Jesus.

The Gentile magi play no further role in Jesus' life until the very end when their counterparts, the centurion "and those with him," make their profession of faith, "Truly this man was God's Son!"—an affirmation of the Gentiles' Christian faith, a faith that is "new."

As Matthew's account continues, the infant Jesus relives events in the history of the Jews: like Moses, he is preserved from an attempt to kill him by the slaughter of male children (2:16–18), and, like the people of Israel, he journeys to and from Egypt (2:19–23). Each step of Matthew's account is shown to be a fulfillment of a Hebrew Bible prophecy (1:23; 2:6, 15, 18, 23). All of this reflects the Jewishness of Matthew.

Though the Matthean community sought to preserve its Jewish heritage, the gospel's harsh condemnation of scribes and Pharisees indicates that the transition from that past to its Gentile future was not without rancor, as we saw above. The break between the Christian community and the synagogue is shown to be foreseen by Jesus: "I tell you, many will come from east and west and will eat with Abraham and Isaac and Jacob in the kingdom of heaven, while the heirs of the kingdom will be thrown into the outer darkness, where there will be weeping and gnashing of teeth" (8:11–12).

7. Summary

The gospel reflects a transition in Matthew's community of Christians in Antioch from an early period when they were part of Judaism to the late first century when they were substantially Gentile. That transition was not an easy one, but they never lost a deep respect for their Jewish heritage as they sought to preserve both the "old" and the "new." If they were, perhaps, less liberal, less Pauline, and more Petrine, more conservative, as time passed, it was an expression of their desire to preserve their heritage, for "They were now adrift in a Gentile sea, headed for a Gentile future" (J. Meier, op. cit. p. 49).

STUDY QUESTIONS

1. What role did Antioch play in the early church?
2. What factions in the Antioch community were represented by Peter and Paul?
3. What were the effects of the disaster of 70 A.D. on the Antioch community?
4. What do we know of the author of Matthew's gospel?
5. What can we surmise about the community for which the gospel was written?
6. What are the sources of the gospel's contents?

7. How does Matthew's treatment of the community's leadership differ from Mark's?
8. What is the relationship between the "old" and the "new" in Matthew?
9. How is this relationship expressed in Matthew's account of Jesus' nativity?

X

The Johannine Communities

A. THE GOSPEL OF JOHN

SUGGESTED READING: THE GOSPEL OF JOHN 1:1–18; 10:1–18; CHAPTERS 14–21

1. The Tradition

Even the most casual reader would immediately note a striking contrast in both style and between the gospel of John and any one of the synoptic gospels, i.e. Mark, Luke, or Matthew. We would expect, then, that another purpose and circumstance lies behind the composition of the fourth gospel. From what we have already seen, we would anticipate finding the gospel's source in a Christian community facing a different challenge from those we have already examined.

The gospel that tradition attributes to "John" reached its final form late in the first century of our era, most likely between 90 and 100 A.D. It also appears to have been edited (or redacted) at least twice, and the final form was completed by a different hand than the one that produced the earlier versions. Since the sources of the gospel are as early as, or even earlier than, the synoptics, it is obvious that we are dealing with a longer period of development when we come to the fourth gospel.

Raymond Brown in his *The Gospel of John,* Vol. I, pp. xxxiv–vi, posits the complex genesis of the gospel's final form. Outlining

Brown's views: the formation of John began with an oral tradition similar to, but not identical with, the one used by the synoptic gospels. One of the sources of this early tradition might well have been an eyewitness to some of the events preserved by the tradition. At a later stage, the tradition was strongly influenced by a single person whose outlook is the one reflected in the first written form of the gospel. It is possible that this unknown "evangelist" could have himself been the author of the transitional edition of John. Though the tradition appears to have been in Aramaic at one time, the first written form of the gospel was in Greek. This particular written version, however, did not record the entire tradition.

Sometime later, between 80 and 90 A.D., this version was reedited by its original author, now confronted with new challenges and opportunities, resulting in a rearrangement of the previous contents. It would appear that such a reworking of John occurred at the time of the definitive break between Christianity and Judaism, followed by the expulsion of the Christians from the synagogues. We have already seen the traumatic results of such an excommunication. These sufferings explain the hostility toward the "Jews" found in the fourth gospel.

Ten to twenty years later, as the century ends, John is given a final redaction by someone, not the original author or editor. Material omitted by earlier forms of the gospel are now included. Examples would be the lengthy discourse following what is the obvious end of the last supper account (15:1–17:26) and the appendix to the gospel (21:1ff). It is possible that this final editor was familiar with the synoptics and incorporated some of that material into John. It should be pointed out that as we have manuscripts only of the gospel's final, turn-of-the-century version, the above is conjecture based on an analysis of that text.

2. The Community

The editorial and redactive process by which John developed gives us an insight into the complex history of the Christian community which is the gospel's source. The letters attributed to "John" will carry our story beyond the final version of the gospel itself. These documents together present us with the unique portrait of a church, or possibly a group of churches, as the first century comes to a close.

At the earliest level of John's development, we find a community of Jewish Christians who accepted Jesus as the messiah promised in the Hebrew Bible and the one whose coming was thought to be near. These Christians maintained their relationship with the synagogues and regarded themselves as part of the Judaism of their day. Among this Jewish sect were likely to have been followers of John the Baptist. The gospel give the impression that one or two of the "witnesses" had been disciples of the Baptist (1:35).

3. The Beloved Disciple

Influential in this early community was the person the gospel refers to repeatedly as "the one whom Jesus loved" (13:23; 19:26; 20:2; 21:7, 20–24). He only appears in the final days of Jesus' life, though his presence is hinted at as a companion of Peter's brother, Andrew (1:35, 40). At the last supper, the beloved disciple is shown as closer to Christ than Peter. In fact, Peter must communicate to Jesus through him (13:24). This disciple is the only one of Jesus' male followers to be present at the crucifixion, and the beloved disciple is the first "believer" after the resurrection (20:8), even though, up to that point, he had not seen the risen Christ. Then, in the appendix to the gospel, we read, "That disciple whom Jesus loved said to Peter, 'It is the Lord!' " (21:7), indicating again a priority of this figure over Peter.

The identity of the beloved disciple is the subject of much debate. He is certainly the "witness" who was most important in the Johannine community, and it was by his authority that John's unique depiction of Jesus becomes part of the community's traditions. The striking differences between the picture of Jesus found in the synoptic gospels and the one in John could be explained by the presence of this eyewitness. Who is he? Raymond Brown, in *The Community of the Beloved Disciple,* p. 35, notes: "[Oscar] Cullman, then, may be right in his long-held theory that we cannot know the name of the beloved disciple, even though we can suspect: 'He is a former disciple of John the Baptist. He began to follow Jesus in Judea when *Jesus himself was in close proximity to the Baptist.* He shared the life of his master during Jesus' last stay in Jerusalem. He was known to the high priest. His connection with Jesus was different from that of Peter, the representative of the Twelve.' "

4. The Newcomers

At some point in these early years another group appears in the Johannine community. Raymond Brown (*The Community of the Beloved Disciple,* pp. 34ff) identifies them as Hellenist Christians, expelled from Jerusalem, who went to Samaria and made converts there. He sees evidence of their existence in the incident of Jesus meeting with the Samaritan women found in John's gospel (4:1ff). Two characteristics of this group are crucial. They were strongly biased against the temple worship, the very focus of the Jewish religion, and they were the source of what is called "high" christology. It was "high" christology that would act as a catalyst for a dramatic change in the community's future.

5. Christology

In "low" christology, Jesus' role is described in terms found either in the Hebrew Bible or among intertestamental expressions, i.e. messiah, prophet, servant, Lord or Son of God. None of these titles, including the last two, indicate any participation in divinity, a notion that Jewish monotheism would certainly have rejected. In the New Testament documents earlier than John, the use of these titles was in line with the earlier tradition. Yet there was an aware-ness that these titles did not adequately deal with the full reality of Jesus. The hymn, quoted by Paul in Philippians 2:6, indicates the belief that there was something transcendent about Jesus, falling short, however, of an expression of his divinity.

The clearest New Testament statement of Jesus' divinity is in the Prologue of John, "In the beginning was the Word . . . and the Word was God" (1:1), but references to it are found elsewhere in the gospel (3:13; 5:37; 8:24, 27, 58; 10:30; 14:9). We can only surmise how such a "high" christology came to be a part of the Johannine tradition. One factor could have been the Samaritan rejection of the messiah as a descendant of David which would have opened the way for another understanding of Jesus' role and nature. He could be seen as one descending from above and who pre-existed before his earthly manifestation. Nevertheless, it must be kept in mind that the fuller understanding of the relationship between the human and the divine in Jesus will only come with the ecumenical councils of the fourth and fifth centuries.

However, there was an immediate result when the Johannine community came under the influence of a "high" christology. Those who held this view of Jesus as sharing in the divine nature would be anathema to the Jews of the synagogue, and this concept probably resulted in their expulsion. However, by now the tragic events of the Jewish wars had taken place, and, as we saw above, Judaism, in its struggle to survive, had become intolerant of any deviation from the Pharisaic position. Expulsion of those Johan-nine Christians from the synagogues seems to have been particu-larly traumatic and must have resulted in a severe persecution of this community which they blamed on the "Jews."

We saw in our discussion of Matthew something of the bitter-ness that resulted when a similar expulsion must have occurred in Antioch. However, in that case the hostility was focused on the Pharisaic leadership. Matthew shows no antipathy toward the Jews as such. In fact, as we pointed out, it is the most Jewish of the gospels. For John, the opponents of Jesus are the "Jews." They plot his death. "It is better for you to have one man die for the people than to have the whole nation destroyed" (11:50). They force a reluctant Pilate to order Jesus' execution. And the Jews pose a threat to the early church (20:19). We can presume that we have here the legacy of a bitter period in the history of the Johannine community.

6. The World

By now, as we approach the end of the century, the reediting of the gospel by its original author has been completed and the alienation between the synagogue and the Johannine church is complete. It is at this time that we detect an ambiguity in the community's attitude toward "the world." In John we are told, "For God so loved the world that he gave his only Son, so that everyone who believes in him may not perish but may have eternal life. Indeed, God did not send the Son into the world to condemn the world, but in order that the world might be saved through him" (3:16–17). Yet we also read, "Those who hate their life in this world will keep it for eternal life" (12:25). "I am asking on their behalf; I am not asking on behalf of the world" (17:9). "I have given them your word, and the world has hated them because they do not belong to the world, just as I do not belong to the world" (17:14).

Such an ambiguity would indicate that at one point the Johannine communities were open to the Hellenistic world around it, welcoming Gentile converts. Then the atmosphere changed, perhaps as a result of being seen as no longer a Jewish sect and being exposed to persecution as an illegal religion. But there may have been more. John is distinctive for its emphasis on the central role of love in the life of the Christian. What might not be noticed is that this love is focused on the fellow members of the community, not outsiders: "I give you a new commandment, that you love one another. Just as I have loved you, you also should love one another" (13:34). The supreme evidence of love is to "lay down one's life for one's *friends*" (15:13). The love of "neighbor" or the love of one's enemies as expressed in the synoptics is not found in John. The community seems to have closed in on itself.

7. The Other Christian Communities

However, the Johannine communities were not completely isolated. There is evidence in the gospel of an attempt at appealing to those Jews who still believed in Christ as the Messiah but were reluctant to leave the synagogues. Raymond Brown (op. cit. p. 71) calls them "crypto-Christians" and believes that the following passage from the gospel refers to them: "Nevertheless many, even of the authorities, believed in him. But because of the Pharisees they did not confess it, for fear that they would be put out of the synagogue; for they loved human glory more than the glory that comes from God" (12:42-43).

A similar hope is expressed that the followers of John the Baptist might transcend their objections to the Johannine communities' "high" christology, though the subordinate position of the Baptist to Jesus is continually stressed. John himself is shown to recognize who Jesus is (1:27, 29-34), though only as "the one who is coming after me" (1:27). Nowhere is there the hostility toward the Baptist's followers that we see John express toward the Jews.

But the contribution of the final redactor, particularly the final section of the gospel (21:1-23), reveals a complex relationship between the Johannine communities and the other Christian churches. It is reflected in the way the "beloved disciple" is contrasted to the chief apostle, Peter.

At the final scene in John by the lakeside the beloved disciple is first to recognize the resurrected Jesus, and he reidentifies him to Peter. Peter, in turn, is given care of the Lord's flock, but admonished to give them tender, loving care. "Love" is the Johannine vision of community rule. The beloved disciple's independence from Peter (21:22) may reflect the somewhat tenuous relationship between the churches that saw their traditions rooted in a Petrine heritage and the Johannine communities which traced their traditions back to the beloved disciple. Was there a rivalry here that isolated the Johannine communities from the main body of Christianity?

B. THE LETTERS OF JOHN

SUGGESTED READING: 1, 2 AND 3 JOHN

1. The Split

As the century ended, a leader in the Johannine communities, who referred to himself as the Presbyter, wrote the three documents we call the letters of John. Such a late date of composition rules out the author's being either the apostle, the beloved disciple, or the evangelist. The author, however, could be the final redactor of John's gospel, but there is no overwhelming evidence that he was.

1 John is more of a religious tract than a letter and might have been destined to circulate among the Johannine churches that shared the views expressed in the gospel. In 2 John, there is mention of "the elect lady" (v. 1), which could simply be the author's way of designating an individual church. 3 John is addressed to "beloved Gaius," someone who exercised responsibility in a Johannine community. We can assume that the letters were written within a limited period of time as they all reflect a similar circumstance.

2. The Cause

What had happened to these communities who shared the traditions found in John? We are told that "Many deceivers have gone out into the world, those who do not confess that Jesus Christ has come in the flesh" (2 Jn 7). "They went out from us, but they did not belong to us; for if they had belonged to us, they would have remained with us. But by going out they made it plain that none of them belongs to us" (1 Jn 2:19). Obviously some members of the Johannine communities have separated from the group for whom the author of the letters is speaking. Moreover, they seem to have been successful in winning converts to their position. "They are from the world; therefore what they say is from the world, and the world listens to them" (1 Jn 4:5).

The Presbyter warns his sister church of one such "progressive" (2 Jn 9). Further, he is not to be welcomed. "Do not receive into the house or welcome [him]," (v. 10), though this seems to be a violation of the fundamental Johannine command, "Let us love one another" (v. 5). If the group addressed in 2 John had been too open, the church leader, Diotrephes, spoken of in 3 John, is being obstructionist, favoring those who are spreading the view to which the Presbyter objects and refusing to welcome those who wish to oppose it, even expelling members of his own church (vv. 9–10). Since both groups in question share the traditions of John, what is the source of the dispute?

1 John tells us, "By this you know the Spirit of God: every spirit that confesses that Jesus Christ has come *in the flesh* is from God, and every spirit that does not confess Jesus is not from God" (4:2–3). Up to this point no one questioned that Jesus was a human being. The debate in the gospel of John was between Christians and Jews and was focused on the divinity of Christ. However, John's stress on the transcendence of Jesus apparently led some of his readers to the conclusion that the humanity of Jesus, his ministry, even his death on the cross, played no role in salvation. The divine dimension of Christ had absorbed the human. The efforts of the gospel to emphasize the intimate relationship between the divine Father and Son led to this unforeseen result. Now a deviation in understanding the tradition which is accepted by one group of

Christians but rejected by the other had led to a schism in the Johannine communities.

3. The Break-Up of the Johannine Communities

What followed? It would appear that the "progressives" mentioned in 2 John (v. 9) were eventually absorbed into other second century heretical sects. They may have brought the gospel of John with them, as this work was popular in such groups of Christians, principally the Gnostics to whom we have already referred. The remainder of the Johannine Christians may have persisted for a time, isolated to some degree from the main body of the church.

However, since the main Christian communities accepted the Johannine gospel and letters as part of their tradition, we can assume that these remaining Johannine communities were accepted as well. It would appear that the author of the letters of John, by his defense of the gospel, succeeded in giving it an orthodox interpretation. Thus we may owe to this nameless Christian leader the fact that the gospel of John and the three letters are a part of the New Testament.

The struggle of the Johannine communities to preserve their tradition in the face of new challenges provides us with a paradigm for future developments in the history of the church. Disagreements on the meaning of the "good news," however well intentioned, frequently give rise to schism and heresy. Of course, these two epithets are what each opponent applies to the other. Neither unity nor uniformity has been a characteristic of the Christian communities since their beginning. Jesus' prayer at the last supper in John, "that they may all be one . . . that they may become completely one" (7:21–23), is a promise for the future, one to be fulfilled at the end of time. In fact, we find a vision of that final event in one of the remaining documents we are to study.

STUDY QUESTIONS

1. How did the gospel of John develop?
2. Describe the original Johannine community. Who was the beloved Disciple?
3. Who were the "newcomers"?
4. What are "high" and "low" christology and what resulted from introduction of the latter into the Johannine community?
5. What was the attitude of the Johannine community toward "the world"?
6. What might have been the relationship between the Johannine community and the main body of Christian communities?
7. What event seems to be reflected in the Johannine letters and what may have been the outcome?

XI

The Final Documents of
The New Testament

A. 2 PETER, JAMES AND JUDE

SUGGESTED READING: THE LETTERS OF 2 PETER, JAMES AND JUDE

Three more letters are included in the New Testament: 2 Peter, James and Jude. These works have several things in common. For one, each is attributed to one of the apostles, though modern scholarship questions such an attribution, feeling that the actual writers are anonymous. Also, the three authors are Hellenized Jews writing in the final years of the first century. James writes for fellow Jewish-Hellenistic Christians, whereas 2 Peter and Jude have in mind a general audience of Christians.

Though the number of Hellenized Jewish Christians may have dwindled as the church approached the turn of the century, there still were many in the Christian communities. This being the case, 2 Peter, James and Jude can give us little specific information about individual churches. We simply know very little about the communities that gave rise to these New Testament documents. In not treating these letters further, we in no way denigrate their value as part of the Christian tradition. As our focus has been on the communities that lie behind the documents of the New Testament, 2 Peter, James and Jude are not much help in this regard.

B. THE BOOK OF REVELATION

SUGGESTED READING: REVELATION, CHAPTERS 2, 3, 21, 22

We now come to the document that concludes our study of the New Testament, a work that fittingly occupies that position since it looks to the end of history. Its title, Revelation, is the English equivalent of the Greek *Apocalypsis.* Of all the documents in the Christian Bible, it is one of the most difficult to understand. An example of what is called "apocalyptic literature," Revelation presents the current conditions of its times and a hoped-for future through a richly symbolic and allegorical language. The author attempts to reveal the true, if mysterious, meaning of the events he and his readers are experiencing. We saw such literature in our discussion of the Hebrew Bible documents from the post-exilic period, most especially the book of Daniel.

Revelation was written to give hope to Christians who were undergoing persecution for their beliefs and presents this oppression as part of a titanic struggle between the forces of good and evil. It promises that, in the end, the beneficent powers will be victorious and the faithful Christians will enjoy the fruits of that triumph. "Then I saw a new heaven and a new earth; for the first heaven and the first earth had passed away. . . . And I saw the holy city, the new Jerusalem, coming down out of heaven from God . . . the home of God is among mortals . . . he will wipe every tear from their eyes. Death will be no more; mourning and crying and pain will be no more, for the first things have passed away" (21:1–4).

There is general agreement that the persecution in question occurred during the reign of Emperor Domitian (81–96 A.D.). If such is the case, it would raise a question about the traditional attribution of this document to the apostle John. In our consideration of the Johannine literature, we have already discussed the relationship of the apostle John to the sources of those documents. Even accepting that the author of Revelation was named John, there is no overwhelming reason to believe that he was connected with any New Testament figure. The author was a Hellenized Jew, but seems to have thought in Aramaic while writing in Greek. Certainly an influential figure, he was exiled to the island of Patmos during the persecutions on which he himself commented.

The churches which Revelation admonishes—Ephesus, Smyrna, Pergamum, Thyatira, Sardis, Philadelphia and Laodicea (2:1–3:22)—are found clustered on the west coast of the Roman province of Asia (the western region of modern Turkey) around ancient Smyrna (modern Izmir). We already know that Ephesus was an early center of Christian influence and Patmos lies just off the coast. All of this indicates that, as the century closed, a group of persecuted Christian communities heard words of encouragement from an imprisoned leader. Unfortunately for our purpose, we can say little more of the church or churches that gave us the final words of the New Testament. "The One who gives this testimony says, 'Surely I am coming soon.' Amen. Come, Lord Jesus!" (22:20–21).

STUDY QUESTIONS

1. What do 2 Peter, James and Jude have in common?
2. What is "apocalyptic" literature, and what is an example of it found in the Hebrew Bible?
3. What appears to have occasioned the writing of Revelation?

XII

Finale

THE CHURCH OF SAN CLEMENTE

In Rome, the Eternal City, and not far from the Colosseum, stands the ancient Church of San Clemente. A medieval structure, it is built upon the ruins of an eleventh century Romanesque basilica. When the area was excavated, the remains of an even earlier place of Christian worship were uncovered—one of the first churches erected in Rome at the beginning of the fourth century, just after Emperor Constantine granted legal status to Christianity. As these early churches were usually built on the places where Christians gathered to worship in secret during persecutions, we can assume that the structure below San Clemente is such a site.

As the area around this earliest of Rome's churches was further excavated, a shrine to Mithra was discovered. An Indo-Iranian god, the worship of Mithra was popular in the empire, particularly among soldiers. The shrine included a temple and an additional structure, part of which was a school. Opposite the shrine, across a narrow street, was the place where, during the same period, Christians were worshiping clandestinely, probably in the private home of a well-to-do Christian which was replaced by the first San Clemente.

Standing in that street, one might try to imagine that street scene some 1,700 years ago in the waning years of the third century. Some of the passers-by would enter the prosperous Mithratic shrine, openly and without fear. Others, fearfully, cautiously and as unobtrusively as possible, would slip into the building opposite to

197

attend a secret gathering of Christians. The contrast could hardly be sharper. Yet, from the perspective of that street in the imperial city, what would have been the observer's expectations for the future? Shrines to Mithra still dot the ruins of the ancient Roman world, yet there is virtually no trace of any overtly Christian structure earlier than the fourth century. The observer would have no reason to believe that Christianity was the more likely to survive.

Assuredly, two centuries earlier, the future of Christianity was even more clouded. The Christian communities we have been studying, already persecuted, faced two more centuries in an illegal and vulnerable status. Yet today there are no active places of worship dedicated to Mithra. The early churches that followed upon those of the first century and one of whose clandestine places of worship lies below San Clemente's were succeeded by the Christians who built shrines that rose out of ruins of the empire itself.

THE ULTIMATE CHALLENGE

The above is not written out of any sense of triumph but rather to emphasize the debt we owe these Christian communities which sprang up as the "witnesses" and moved out into the empire after the death and resurrection of Jesus. Spreading the good news from the mideast to Rome and beyond, they were fulfilling the command of the risen Christ himself, "Go therefore and make disciples of all nations . . . teaching them to obey everything that I have commanded you" (Mt 28:19–20). Paul's career as a "witness" is the best known to us, but there were others also, and we have no reason to doubt that many of them gave their lives as well in the pursuit of their mission.

At the close of the apostolic age, the early Christians faced the challenge of preserving the traditions entrusted to them. An authoritative leadership took the place of the now-departed "witnesses." But there was an awareness that the leadership provided by the "elders" and "overseers" would not be sufficient in itself to preserve the traditions of the churches facing newer and differing circumstances. It would be Jesus himself who would remain with his church to protect it. "And remember, I am with you always, to the end of the age" (Mt 28:20). In time, this protective presence was seen as that of the Spirit. "When the Spirit of truth comes, he will guide you into all the truth" (Jn 16:13).

THE ADVENT OF THE NEW TESTAMENT

In our consideration of the New Testament, we must not forget that the early Christian communities treasured the heritage they had received from Israel. The Hebrew Bible was the "scriptures" mentioned in virtually every document we have studied. "For whatever was written in former days was written for our instruction, so that by steadfastness and by the encouragement of the scriptures we might have hope" (Rom 15:4). Even though the Christian and Jewish communities became alienated from one another, the churches never repudiated their heritage. The scrolls that formed the Septuagint were certainly valued possessions of the Christian churches.

During the apostolic age, the letters of Paul, painstakingly copied and recopied, were circulated among the Pauline communities. A letter sent to one community or group of communities would be shared among all the churches. As the sub-apostolic period opened, additional letters, attributed to Paul, were also in circulation. The gospel of Mark, that crucially important document, appeared. It is possible that it originated in Rome. Then, within a few years, came the gospels of Luke and Matthew, strongly influenced by that of Mark. They in their turn were circulated from community to community.

By the century's end, a virtual library of documents emerged among the Christian churches of the mideast, northern Africa, Asia Minor, and southern Europe. Now included in these collections were the Acts of the Apostles, companion volume to Luke's gospel, the gospel of John, the Johannine letters, letters attributed to Peter, James and Jude, and two unique works, the letter to the Hebrews and the book of Revelation. However, not every collection contained the same documents.

Other Christian documents were also in existence. Some were earlier forms of the later works we have already seen; others we know nothing about. We can surmise their existence, but they are lost to history. Several documents we have are possibly sub-apostolic, but never became part of the collection later to be called the "New Testament." One such is the Didache; another is a letter from Clement of Rome, and from the very end of the period we have the letters of Ignatius of Antioch. These are examples of non-biblical, early Christian literature.

Among the churches at the beginning of the second century (even though all the documents that would form the Christian Bible were in existence) there was no general agreement on what was to be included in the New Testament. Churches simply had varying collections of sacred scrolls. In fact, it is not until the fourth century that we find groups of churches reaching definitive conclusions on just which works were to be added to the Greek Hebrew Bible, the Septuagint, to form the sacred scriptures of the church. Though isolated variations persisted, it is the makeup of the Bible as used by Christians today. Interestingly, the oldest Bibles in book or codex form in existence now date from the fourth century.

PRESERVING THE TRADITIONS

We saw how the Hebrew Bible rose out the experiences of a people as they moved through history. Individual authors, editors and redactors recorded what the people came to believe was God's message as revealed through what had happened to them. The Hebrew Bible preserved the religious traditions of Israel from that time to the present day. We also saw how these traditions became part of the Christian heritage as well.

Though the time span was very much shorter and the people far more ethnically diverse, a similar process brought the New Testament into existence. In this case, the traditions, the "good news," arose from the life and words of Jesus, the Nazarene, as experienced by the "witnesses." During the apostolic age, the men and women carried the "gospel" to what became the earliest Christian communities. Made up of Jews and Gentiles, of the slave and the free, these "churches" experienced what it meant to live the "good news," day by day, in milieus friendly, indifferent and hostile. Out of these lives, recorded by authors, editors and redactors, known and unknown, came the traditions we find in the New Testament.

THE WORD OF GOD

In the Bible, the reader, believer or unbeliever, can find a wealth of history even though the Bible is not meant to be a history text. It is the record of a vast panorama of human experience without parallel. The variety of literary forms it contains is somewhat bewildering, and each must be read in the light of our knowledge about such forms—at times, a formidable task. However, for the believer, Jew and Christian alike, the Bible is the word of God. In the complex process of the Bible's development, Yahweh preserved his message as a tradition that would guide the faithful reader in the effort to do God's will. For the guidance of the Christian, the Bible contains the tradition, the "good news," which is the message of Jesus, the Christ.

From what has been said, those who accept the Bible as the word of God have also placed their trust in a process that extends back nearly four millennia, almost to the dawn of history, to the men and women who first believed in Yahweh and sought to do his will. In that initial trust, kept alive by tradition, is the "tap root" of the biblical faith for both Jew and Christian. The latter, however, looks back also to another group who, within the Jewish faith, first believed that Jesus of Nazareth was the fulfillment of the promises they found in the Hebrew Bible. The word of God is not simply ours, it is theirs. Their faith, the faith of the people and of the churches, expressed and preserved in various documents we have studied, has made ours possible.

NOTES

1. Both Matthew (2:1) and Luke (1:5) agree that Herod the Great ruled Judea at the time of Jesus' birth. Herod's death is known to be in 4 B.C. Jesus would have been born most likely in the previous year.
2. "By way of a very broad approximation, about 90% of critical scholarship judges that Paul did not write the Pastorals (Timothy 1 and 2 and Titus), 80% that he did not write Ephesians, and 60% that he did not write Colossians" (Raymond E. Brown, *The Churches the Apostles Left Behind,* p. 47).
3. The English word "priest" stems from the Greek "presbyteros." However, this English word usually refers to the central figure in a religious ritual such as a sacrifice. The Hebrew and Greek words for such a person are, respectively, "kohen" and "hiereus." There is no evidence that Jesus of Nazareth ever applied such a "sacral" title to either himself or his followers. Given the place the priesthood occupied in the Jewish and Gentile religions, again it does not seem likely that the early Christian communities would have given that title to their leadership.

Appendix A

INTRODUCTION

Modern physics and related sciences explore the origins of our universe. Biology, anthropology, and archeology can give us insights into the origin and evolution of mankind and human society. As noted earlier, it is between the conclusions of these sciences and the biblical account of such origins that much controversy originates. Is it possible to reconcile the differences? The following two articles are an attempt to do so.

BANG, YOU'RE ALIVE

Billions of years ago there occurred an explosion of energy from a single, incredibly dense point. All the reality we know, including ourselves, resulted from that "big bang." This expansion did not occur in time or in space but rather marked the beginning of both time and space. Nor was the expansion uniform. Its variations gave rise to strange entities with strange sounding names—quarks, gravitons, gluons, even anti-quarks. These entities existed for only the first thousandth of a second before coalescing into the primary building blocks of the stars, the protons, neutrons and electrons.

He is frail. Made virtually helpless by Lou Gehrig's disease, unable to speak save via a computer and a voice-synthesizer, yet the mind of Dr. Stephen W. Hawkins ranges through the vastnesses of human knowledge to its frontiers. He has been called the most brilliant theoretical physicist since Einstein. In his book, *A Brief History of Time,* Dr. Hawkins makes the following observation: "... an early generation of stars first had to form. These stars converted some of the original hydrogen and helium into elements like carbon and oxygen, out of which we are made. The stars then exploded as supernovas, and their debris went to form other stars and planets, among them those of our solar system, which is about five thousand million years old. The first one or two thousand million years of the earth's existence were too hot for the development of anything complicated. The remaining three thousand million years or so have been taken up by the slow process of biological evolution, which has led from the simplest organisms to beings who are capable of measuring time back to the big bang" (p. 124).

To this brief summary, every branch of science has contributed. It is the summation of millennia of research and experimentation going back to those who first plotted the movements of the heavenly lights, to those who created such primitive observatories as Stonehenge (England) and El Caracole (Yucatan). This vision of our universe and its creation is a magnificent achievement of the human imagination which, after all, is itself a product of this creative process. " 'Why is the universe the way we see it?' The answer then is simple: If it had been different, we would not be here" (ibid. p. 125).

But our understanding of reality is not limited to scientific discoveries. In the search for truth, our imagination has a far wider range and can express itself in other ways. Symbols and myths, for instance, can be better suited to capturing the meaning of some of our experiences, religious experience being a case in point. Religions universally make use of symbols and myths. The error is to assume such a usage implies falsehood, something we do all too frequently. Aesop's fables actually contain shrewd observations of human behavior. Charles Dickens' stories contain a greater store of the knowledge of human psychology than most scientific tracts on that subject. When the people of the Bible began to express their religious heritage they made use of the wealth of myths found in the tribal memory.

As we saw in recounting their history, the people of the Bible originated in the eastern region of ancient Mesopotamia. The culture they first experienced was that of the Sumerians whose myths reflected the world around them. The Tigris and Euphrates rivers, on which the Sumerians depended for their existence, were notably erratic, flooding and drying up in turn. From the mountain ranges to the north and east came cold winds and raging storms. Hot, dry winds blew out of the deserts to the south, whereas pleasant, cool breezes arose from the Mediterranean in the west. The Sumerians were also aware of the great bodies of water that lay to the south and west of them, waters that could be calm at one moment and turbulent the next. It is not difficult to see why they would conceive of their universe as a chaos out of which a bit of understandable order had been created, and that tenuously.

Other elements in their mythology may have even deeper roots. We were never nocturnals. From our dim past, we inherit a fear of the dark. In the times when only the flickering light of a fire, torch or primitive oil lamp would dispel the darkness, it was all the more oppressive and the gift of light was the more appreciated. It was the largess of the gods. For the Sumerians the creation of light marked the triumph of order over chaos. And their pantheon of deities was responsible for every aspect of reality, a reality caught up in the titanic struggle between the gods. Humanity was a by-product of this celestial imbroglio. These myths formed the heritage of the people of the Bible.

However, the religious experiences of the people of the Bible over the centuries had been much different than those of the Sumerians, and so they revamped their inheritance to better express the reality they knew. For these people there was no pantheon of warring deities. There was one God, and it was he who brought order to the chaos. The words are those of the *Priestly* tradition: In the beginning when God created the heavens and the earth, the earth was a formless void and darkness covered the face of the deep, while a wind from God swept over the face of the waters. Then God said, 'Let there be light' " (Gen 1:1–3).

The creative acts that follow are an example of demythologizing. The sky once seen as the abode of the gods is now a mere bowl or dome separating the waters of the chaos. The stars and planets, the heavenly bodies, once the thrones of the gods, points from which they exercised their powers, are now luminaries which measure the passage of time. The polytheism of the Sumerians and the other surrounding cultures is specifically repudiated in the description of creation found in Genesis.

Genesis also departs from its Sumerian sources in another important respect. After the first act of creation we are told, "God saw that the light was good" (1:4). This is repeated no less than five times as the account of creation continues. Finally, when God surveys his handiwork, we are told, "God saw everything that he had made, and indeed, it was very good" (1:31). We have here a crucial innovation. For the Sumerians and for many cultures contemporary with that of the people of the Bible, reality was dualistic, made up of good and evil principles at war with each other. Evil was as real as good. But if the God of the Hebrew Bible is the only God and he is good, then all that he creates must be good as well. Let us turn to the beginning of the human story, starting with the scientific version.

Every few years—at times, every few months—it seems discoveries are made which enlighten us about our ancestors, both human and pre-human. Our roots extend back almost four million years but they may be properly called human for only about half that time. Evidence of culture begins some 100,000 years ago. And it was but 30,000 years in the past that the hunting-gathering tribes moved into villages, probably with the advent of agriculture. It was the growth of trade between these villages that gave rise to a written language. Soon villages, here and there, became large enough to be called cities. At this point we have civilization, properly speaking. In very broad strokes, this is the scientific vision of our origins.

Turning to the Bible, we see again how it contrasts with the contemporary myths. The Sumerian epic, Enuma Elish, pictured humankind as arising from a mixture of the remains of a defeated, evil deity and the clay of the earth—an intrinsically flawed being, forever at the mercy of a power struggle between competing gods and goddesses. How different is the vision of Genesis.

"Then God said, 'Let us make humankind in our image, according to our likeness; and let them have dominion over the fish of the sea, and over the birds of the air, and over the cattle, and over all the wild animals of the earth, and over every creeping thing that creeps upon the earth'" (1:26).

Again, the effect is to demythologize. The realms of the sky, the ocean and the land, once seen as the domains of rival gods, are now placed into human hands. Most importantly, there is nothing standing between ourselves and our creator, no pantheon of divinities ruling our daily lives often like petty tyrants. Nor should we fail to note that the human role is shared by both the male and female, an equality rarely expressed in cultures contemporary with the Bible.

Must a choice now be made between these two visions of the human origins: the biblical and the scientific? Here several matters must be raised. Every vision of reality, whether scientific or religious, arises from the human imagination inspired by a faith or trust. The scientist trusts that his investigations, experiments, trials and tests do reveal truths about reality. It is a matter of faith because there is no way to demonstrate this premise. No test can prove the validity of tests. Similarly, the religious truths which the people of the Bible expressed via the myths and symbols of Genesis are accepted as true by the faithful reader. They too cannot be demonstrated.

Evolution itself is often referred to as a theory or hypothesis, and correctly so. It is proposed to explain the vast array of fossil evidence that has been gathered, evidence that clearly indicates the appearances of new forms of life over millions of years. The discoveries of the role of genetics in producing life forms gives us a clue to the mechanism of the evolutionary process. Like all scientific theories, evolution stands or falls on its success in accounting for the evidence. Under this criterion, evolution certainly stands.

If evolution stands, does not what was described in the opening lines of this chapter rule out "creation" by a divinity? Is evolution incompatible with creation? Why should it be? Evolution is a theory accounting for the process by which things around us come into being—why they are the way they are. As such the hypothesis says nothing about the ultimate source of reality. In fact, those who hold to this scientific vision of our origins and to the belief in a creative God can only marvel at the vastness, intricacy and beauty of what he has achieved.

Of course there is a problem. It began when Darwin first ventured his ideas of human origins. How can evolution be reconciled to the account of Genesis? Obviously, if one takes the biblical account literally, such a reconciliation is impossible. However, as I have already pointed out, such an approach fails to understand both the literary form and the aim of Genesis. Thus the scientist may accept the religious truths of Genesis. The Christian may share the scientific view of human origins. Each vision is an exploration by the human imagination of reality. Is it possible that these two strivings to understand ourselves and our universe might converge in the end? "Then we shall all, philosophers, scientists, and just ordinary people, be able to take part in the discussion of the question of why it is that we and the universe exist. If we find the answer to that, it would be the ultimate triumph of human reason—for then we would know the mind of God" (Hawkins, op. cit. p. 175).

The preamble to the story of God's saving actions is now complete, and we are once again at the beginning of the history of the people of the Bible. We can see how the religious insights gained by the descendants of Abraham some thirteen centuries later were incorporated into the stories of their origins. They learned that there was but one God and his name was Yahweh. Unlikely as the choice might seem, they became his chosen people, the means by which his salvation would reach all mankind. The need for salvation is vividly portrayed in the opening stories of Genesis.

SOMETHING WENT WRONG

In one respect at least, the world of the Sumerians resembled ours; there was little peace. Like the hunting-gathering tribes and the villages before them, the cities and the nascent empires were almost constantly at war. The chaos that surrounded their world was reflected in human society. Their explanation for this mixture of good and evil in reality was to posit the existence of dual principles, one good and one evil and locked in constant struggle. Nature, the gods, humanity, all were affected by this dualism.

In time the people of the Bible came to reject this dualism. If Yahweh was the only God and the one who proclaimed that the universe was "good," then no evil principle could exist. But evil did exist! Genesis, chapters two through eleven, shows the answer to this dilemma. Again, we see that the solution lies in demythologizing their Sumerian heritage.

The second chapter of Genesis (2:4ff) is taken from the Yahwist tradition, much older than the Priestly tradition found in the passage that opens the Hebrew Bible. Its primitive character is evidenced by the more liberal use of Sumerian symbolism—an imaginary geography, marvelous rivers, a garden of delights, a tree of life, a wise and clever snake that walks upright, fearsome, winged cherubim, half human, half animal, wielding a flaming sword.

In Sumerian mythology, the first human is formed from common clay mixed with the blood of a defeated god to bestow life. Genesis reflects this, but with an important difference. "The Lord God formed man from the dust of the ground, and breathed into his nostrils the breath of life; and the man became a living being" (2:7).

The general view of the semitic peoples, even today, is that mankind is composed of matter animated by the Spirit (breath) of God. In death, the "breath of life" is withdrawn and the body returns to its original state. "You are dust, and to dust you shall return" (3:19). The idea of an existing soul is a notion found in the Greek culture. It occurs in the Bible only where the influence of Hellenism is seen.

Before we move from this more primitive account of human creation, another aspect of it should be mentioned. "So the Lord God caused a deep sleep to fall upon the man, and he slept; then he took one of his ribs and closed up its place with flesh. And the rib that the Lord God had taken from the man he made into a woman" (2:21–22).

What motivates the Lord God to create woman is the need of Adam (the word simply means "the man") for a "a helper as his partner" (2:20), the previous creation not having met that necessity. This unity is given further stress when Adam says, "This at last is bone of my bones and flesh of my flesh" (2:23). Again this equality contrasts with contemporary cultures wherein women were considered to be inferior creations.

Now the stage has been set and the cast assembled for the dramatic presentation of the first sin, the introduction of evil into the garden of Eden. It has the elements of a folk tale, including the clever animal who can speak. Only later is Eden's "snake" identified as Satan or the devil. There are echoes of earlier Sumerian myths concerning mankind's fall. However, where the Sumerians seem to hint that the "original sin" was sexual in character, Genesis describes the temptation as the desire "to be like God" (3:5). Human aspirations to be godlike are not uncommon in primitive mythologies. However, for the people of the Bible such an aspiration would have been the ultimate act of human pride, a direct challenge to the supremacy of Yahweh.

The result of this primary sin shared by both the man and the woman is to introduce the paradigmatic disorders into human experience. The first is the loss of innocence; they now experience the need to cover themselves. The earth that once gave of its bounty freely will from now on yield that wealth only with great difficulty. Paralleling that, women will now bring forth children in pain. Summing up the tragedy is the expulsion from the "garden of delights," and all possibility of return is barred by the dreaded cherubim.

From the mythical world of Adam and Eve, Genesis now takes us to the next level of disorder. Here the sin is fratricide, motivated by jealously. The innocent victim, Abel, is a shepherd whose sacrifice pleases God, and the murderer, Cain, is a farmer whose cereal offering does not. This reflects the history of the people of the Bible who for most of their history were herdsmen, driving their flocks along the trade routes of the Middle East. We have only to recall the range wars of our own west to understand the hostility that resulted when the shepherds (in our case, the cattlemen) came into contact with the farmers bent on protecting their fields and crops, a reflection of similar hostility between herdsmen and farmers.

As we proceed in Genesis, the prejudices of a nomadic, rural people are further revealed. Cain is the founder of a city, and his sons are the originators of such civilized things as music (Jubal) and metallurgy (Tubal-cain). Flowing from Cain, then, is the corruption that will now engulf the world until only one man and his family are worthy to be saved from the total destruction that God is to visit upon his creation.

General flooding of the Tigris and Euphrates basin must have occurred several times, giving rise to myths about the total inundation of the world. Such a story is found on a clay tablet discovered in the ruins of Nineveh. The tale of Noah and his ark in Genesis is actually a careful editing of two similar accounts. It is seen as Yahweh's attempt at a new beginning, but the result is simply another "original sin."

Upon leaving the ark, Noah becomes the first vintner and, apparently, the first to overindulge in the product and pass out (9:20). His son, Ham, sees the embarrassing condition of his father, but instead of concealing the fact he noises it abroad. His brothers, in contrast, make every effort to preserve their father's reputation.

Ham is cursed for his sin by Noah. The resulting division is not only between father and son. Ham is the ancestor of the Canaanites, one day to be the implacable enemies of Israel. The progression is intentional: man against God, brother against brother, son against father. Now we are prepared for the climactic scene.

Still today, in the dusty wastes of Mesopotamia, are the ruins of the great civilizations that once prospered there. Among these ruins are the enormous, man-made mounds that are the remains of great towers called ziggurats. These artificial mountains, topped by temples, dominated the first great metropolises of Asia Minor. They were probably inspired by the ancient belief that the dwelling place of the gods was located atop mountains. It was no doubt the memory of the ziggurats that lies behind the story of the tower of Babel. Again, human pride offers a challenge to Yahweh. "Come, let us build ourselves a city, and a tower with its top in the heavens, and let us make a name for ourselves; otherwise we shall be scattered abroad upon the face of the whole earth" (11:4).

The "city of man," with its tower reaching to the level of the divine, is for Genesis the ultimate blasphemy and provokes the final punishment, total disunity. Yahweh frustrates this human effort by confusing the language of the builders, "so that they will not understand one another's speech" (11:7). The "original sin" has now borne its final fruit, total human alienation.

The final vision of the human condition we find in Genesis prior to God's saving action is not all that different from our own. Wars and rumors of war, marching armies, devastation, refugees, and tyrants marred their world and threatened its existence as they do ours. (As I write vast armies gather in the Middle East, engaged in battle.) Like the people of the Bible we feel that it shouldn't be this way. There is the persistent dream of a golden age. For some it lies in the past, but for others it is a hope for the future. This dream to be one day freed from the curse of Babel is the dream of the people of the Bible.

Appendix B

THE SYNOPTIC QUESTION

Of the 661 verses in the gospel of Mark, 80% are repeated in Matthew and 65% are used by Luke, though the latter makes use of the material with considerably more freedom than the former. There is little of Mark not found in the other two gospels that, with Mark, make up the "synoptic gospels." Also, the gospels of Matthew and Luke share some 220 verses which are not Markan. Thus, Matthew and Luke both have a body of unique material, whereas Mark has very little. There are several ways of dealing with what is called the "synoptic question." You can find them detailed in full in "The New Jerome Commentary," pages 587ff. What I outline here is known as the "two source" theory which has the advantage of both simplicity and wide acceptance.

In this view, the gospel of Mark was written first (before 70 A.D.). Both Matthew and Luke had the earlier gospel at hand in writing their gospels later in the first century. The other body of material these later two synoptic gospels put to use consists of a collection of Jesus' sayings. It is customary to call this source "Q" from the German word for "source," "Quelle." It is much debated whether "Q" ever existed as a separate document or whether, for Matthew and Luke, it was simply a shared oral tradition. One of the Gnostic documents found at Nag Hammadi and dated from the second century, called "The Gospel of Thomas," is a collection of sayings purported to be those of Jesus. Though certainly not "Q,"

"Thomas" does argue for the existence of "Q" as a written tradition—one which did not survive, however.

Matthew and Luke wrote their gospels by combining these "two sources," Mark and "Q," with their unique traditions. The resulting resemblances and differences between the synoptic gospels will be most helpful in the effort to discover something about their respective communities. I have diagramed the interrelationship between the sources and the gospels below.

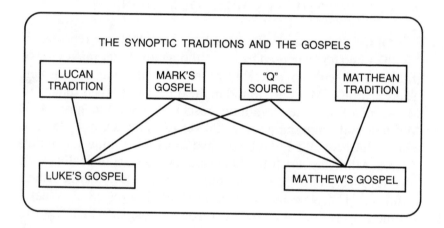

Reading List

COMMENTARIES

The Catholic Study Bible, The New American Bible (New York and Oxford: Oxford University Press, 1990). The Introductory Articles and Reading Guides are particularly helpful.

The New Jerome Biblical Commentary (Englewood Cliffs: Prentice-Hall, 1990). A new and updated edition of a standard reference work.

RESOURCE BOOKS

Boadt, Lawrence, *Reading the Old Testament: An Introduction* (Mahwah: Paulist Press, 1984). Very thorough and useful either individually or in a study group.

Brown, Raymond E., and John P. Meier, *Antioch & Rome* (Mahwah: Paulist Press, 1983). The two centers of early Christianity are carefully recreated by these scholars.

Brown, Raymond E., *The Birth of the Messiah* (Garden City: Doubleday, 1977). Most helpful in comparing the gospels of Matthew and Luke.

————*The Churches the Apostles Left Behind* (Mahwah: Paulist Press, 1984). An excellent depiction of the earliest Christian communities.

————*The Community of the Beloved Disciple* (Mahwah: Paulist Press, 1979). Superb resource on the Johannine community.

————*The Gospel According to John, Anchor Bible, Vol. 29* (Garden City: Doubleday, 1966). The Introduction to the two volume work is the seminal work on the Johannine corpus.

de Vaux, Roland, *Ancient Israel* (New York: McGraw-Hill, 1961). A classic by one of the pioneers of Near Eastern studies. Very detailed and technical, but gives the reader a clear picture of research behind the conclusions arrived at in biblical research.

Friedman, Richard Elliott, *Who Wrote the Bible?* (New York: Summit Books, 1987). A short, readable introduction to Old Testament study. His conclusions are not shared by all.

Hawkins, Stephen W., *A Brief History of Time* (New York: Bantam Books, 1986). An interesting and provocative account of the origin of the universe.

McKenzie, John L., *Dictionary of the Bible* (New York: Macmillan, 1965). For the quick and concise answer to your questions, it can't be beat.

Pagels, Elaine, *The Gnostic Gospels* (New York: Vintage Books, 1989). An introduction to the controversies still being raised by the Gnostic material discovered at Nag Hammadi.

Perkins, Pheme, *Reading the New Testament* (Mahwah: Paulist Press, 1978). A very helpful guide to the New Testament documents, again for both the individual and the group.